Praise for *Soul Leadership*

"I was only a few pages into Dr. Steve Robinson's newest book, *Soul Leadership,* when I found myself thinking about one of my favorite quotes from an old classic, *The Wounded Healer*: "Thus, nothing can be written about ministry without a deeper understanding of the ways in which ministers can make their own wounds available as a source of healing." I'm deeply grateful for spiritual leaders such as Steve Robinson and the late Henri Nouwen who deeply understand at both an experiential and a theological level how empathy and compassion are keystones in the Jesus-shaped pathway to human healing and restoration."

—**LISA HARPER**, author, Bible teacher, and host of *Lisa Harper's Back Porch Theology* podcast

"The enemy doesn't just attack your ministry—he attacks your mind and your soul. In *Soul Leadership*, Dr. Steve Robinson equips leaders with the tools to find healing and strength in Christ. This book is a timely weapon for every leader who wants to finish well."

—**JENTEZEN FRANKLIN**, senior pastor of Free Chapel and *New York Times* bestselling author

"*Soul Leadership* cuts through the noise of performance-driven leadership and calls us back to the heart of what truly matters—leading from a soul made whole. Pastor Steve Robinson offers a rare blend of vulnerability and biblical truth, equipping leaders to thrive both in ministry and the marketplace without losing the essence of who they are."

—**CHAD VEACH**, lead pastor of ZOE Church

"Leadership is a marathon, not a sprint—and the soul is the engine that carries us to the finish line. In *Soul Leadership*, Steve gives us the tools to run with endurance and finish strong. This book is a field guide for leaders who want to leave a lasting legacy."

—**MARK BATTERSON**, *New York Times* bestselling author of *The Circle Maker*

"We live in a culture where many leaders have learned to lead others but ignore the leadership of their own soul. In *Soul Leadership*, Dr. Steve Robinson offers a compelling and grace-filled invitation to reverse that trend. He integrates spiritual depth, emotional awareness, and practical wisdom in a way that helps leaders lead from wholeness rather than exhaustion, chaos, and crisis. As a clinical psychologist, I found this book both grounding and transformative—a guide for anyone who desires to lead with integrity, presence, and soul health."

—**DR. ANDY YARBOROUGH**, clinical psychologist and founder of The Well Clinic

"In *Soul Leadership*, Dr. Steve Robinson gives voice to the struggles so many leaders quietly carry and offers a way forward that brings real restoration. This book doesn't just encourage, it reorients us toward Jesus as the true source of strength, reminding us that when the soul is renewed, leadership becomes life-giving again."

—**TIM TIMBERLAKE**, senior pastor of Celebration Church and author of *The Art of Overcoming*

"I've had the privilege of walking with Steve Robinson for years—seeing his life up close, both in ministry and in the moments that really matter. What I love about Steve is that he doesn't just preach these principles—he lives them. In *Soul Leadership*, Steve has written something special. With transparency, biblical truth, and wisdom earned through the hard places, he helps us see that leadership isn't just about skill or strategy; it's about the soul. He shines a light on what's really behind so many of our struggles as leaders that's not just the pressure around us, but the pain within us. This isn't just another leadership book; it's a road map toward healing, wholeness, and hope. Through the Soul Leadership Cycle, Steve gives us tools to face our wounds, build resilience, and lead from a place of strength and authenticity. Every chapter breathes with encouragement that your pain doesn't disqualify you, it actually qualifies you to lead with greater compassion and depth. If you want to lead stronger, love deeper, and build teams that thrive, this book is a must-read."

—**DINO RIZZO**, executive director of the Association of Related Churches

"The greatest test of leadership is not how you start, but how you finish. In *Soul Leadership*, Dr. Steve Robinson reminds us that lasting leadership begins with a healthy soul anchored in Christ. This book is a needed word for every pastor and leader today."

—**DR. JACK GRAHAM**, senior pastor of Prestonwood Baptist Church

"*Soul Leadership* cuts through symptoms and goes to the source of problems so many leaders face—their own unaddressed trauma. With personal wisdom and professional insight, Steve Robinson reveals how to experience more peace, grace, freedom, and joy as you live out your God-given purpose. This book offers healing and wholeness for anyone who wants to lead like Jesus."

—**CHRIS HODGES**, chancellor of Highlands College, founding pastor of Church of the Highlands, and author of *Pray First* and *Breathe Again*

"Steve is one of my spiritual sons, so I know firsthand how valuable this profound and timely book truly is. *Soul Leadership* is packed with wisdom forged in the fire of real ministry. If you want to leave a lasting legacy for generations to come, this book will help you lead with authenticity, health, and purpose."

—**THOMAS D. MULLINS**, PhD, founding pastor of Christ Fellowship Church

"We live in a pandemic of unprocessed trauma and stress. What gets suppressed will eventually be expressed in painful, harmful ways. Dr. Steve Robinson has provided all of us an evidence-based, research-rich, trauma-informed guide for working through the complex, nuanced journey of moving from unprocessed trauma and stress to wholehearted resilience. Every therapist, life coach, pastor, influencer, and individual should have *Soul Leadership* on their must-read short list."

—**JIM CRESS**, licensed professional counselor and executive advisory board member of the American Association of Christian Counselors

"The future of the Church depends on leaders who are both Spirit-empowered and soul-healthy. In *Soul Leadership*, Dr. Steve Robinson provides timeless wisdom and practical guidance to help leaders thrive. This book is a valuable contribution to the body of Christ and to leadership today."

—**DR. BILLY WILSON**, president of Oral Roberts University, global chair of Empowered21, and chair of Pentecostal World Fellowship

"Great leaders build great teams—but healthy leaders build lasting impact. *Soul Leadership* is a powerful reminder that leadership starts within. Dr. Steve Robinson helps you lead with purpose, passion, and integrity—from the inside out. This is a must-read!"

—**JON GORDON**, eighteen—time bestselling author of *The One Truth* and *The Power of Positive Leadership*

"*Soul Leadership* bridges the gap between spiritual formation and trauma-informed leadership practice. With clarity and compassion, Dr. Steve Robinson helps leaders attend to the inner life so they can lead with integrity and resilience. I am grateful for this timely resource."

—**REV. CHRIS ADAMS**, PhD, Flourishing in Ministry, Rosemead School of Psychology, Biola University

"The greatest move of God always begins in the hidden place of the soul. In *Soul Leadership*, Dr. Steve Robinson calls leaders back to the presence of Jesus, where healing and power are found. This book carries a timely word for a generation of leaders who long to see revival."

—**RUSSELL EVANS**, senior pastor of Planetshakers

"I've walked with Pastor Steve for many years and have seen first-hand the integrity, perseverance, and grit behind this message. *Soul Leadership* isn't theory; it's biblical principles, proven wisdom, and practical help from someone whose life bears the fruit of unwavering faith in Jesus. More than a resource—this is a mentoring moment for every leader who wants to leave a legacy and finish well."

—**DR JEFF LITTLE**, lead pastor of Milestone Church

"My friend Steve Robinson has given us a gift in *Soul Leadership*. He doesn't just describe the impact of trauma on leadership—he shows us how to grow through it. I know leaders at every level will find hope and healing in these pages."

—**GREG SURRATT**, founding pastor of Seacoast Church

"The church needs leaders who don't just build ministries but live with integrity and wholeness as well. Dr. Steve truly models that kind of living. *Soul Leadership* is a timely reminder that when the soul is healthy, everything else flourishes. I thank God for this book and the impact it will have."

—**TOMMY BARNETT**, Dream City Church, Los Angeles Dream Center

"Dr. Steve Robinson's *Soul Leadership* is a vital resource for leaders feeling the weight of unprocessed pain. With personal insight and groundbreaking research, Dr. Robinson's Soul Leadership Cycle offers a practical path to recognize trauma's triggers, build resilience, and grow through God's grace. This book is a lifeline for pastors and executives ready to lead from a healed heart."

—**AARON BURKE**, lead pastor of Radiant Church

"Dr. Steve Robinson has done a remarkable job helping leaders understand why we sometimes think, feel, and act in ways that don't align with our core beliefs or true identity. Whether you lead a team, a family, or simply yourself, Soul Leadership offers profound insights that will help you better understand the connection between your inner world and your leadership. Even if you're unaware of past or present trauma in your life, I encourage you to read at least the first chapter; you won't stop there."

—**DANIEL HARKAVY**, founder of Building Champions and SetPath

Soul
LEADERSHIP

Soul LEADERSHIP

REBOUND FROM CRISIS,
GROW IN RESILIENCE,
LIVE FROM WHOLENESS

DR. STEVE ROBINSON

Soul Leadership: Rebound from Crisis, Grow in Resilience, Live from Wholeness

Published by Maxwell Leadership Publishing, an imprint of Forefront Books, Nashville, Tennessee.
Distributed by Simon & Schuster.

Library of Congress Control Number: Applied For

Print ISBN: 979-8-88710-054-8
E-book ISBN: 979-8-88710-055-5

Cover Design by Studio Gearbox
Interior Design by Bill Kersey, KerseyGraphics

Printed in the United States of America

26 27 28 29 30 31 RR4 10 9 8 7 6 5 4 3 2 1

Dedication

To my wife, Jennifer—

Your love, strength, and steady faith have anchored me through every storm. Thank you for walking alongside me in my healing journey. I'm grateful for your belief in me—I wouldn't be the man, husband, father, or leader I am without you.

To my children, who continue to inspire me and make me proud—I love you deeply, and I pray you always lead from a place of health, humility, and holy dependence on God.

Contents

Foreword

Some books inspire you. Some books inform you. But few books do both. *Soul Leadership* is one of the few.

I've had the privilege of knowing Steve Robinson for more than twenty years. I can tell you without hesitation—he's the real deal. He's a gifted communicator, a trusted pastor, and a resilient leader. But what I admire most about Steve isn't what he's accomplished—it's how he's allowed God to shape his soul along the way.

Most leaders don't burn out because of what's happening around them. They burn out because of what's happening within them. The challenges we never process. The weight we try to carry alone. And too often, we don't recognize it until something breaks.

That's why this book matters.

Steve doesn't write from theory—he writes from experience. He's led through crises, shouldered heavy responsibilities, and walked the long road of healing. He's done the hard inner work required to lead from a place of strength and wholeness—and now he's inviting you to do the same.

One of the things I love most about *Soul Leadership* is how it's built on both practical research and biblical truths. It's for people who are tired of pretending and ready to get real. If you've ever felt the pressure to look strong on the outside while silently falling apart on the inside, this book is for you.

Steve introduces a powerful framework—the Soul Leadership Cycle—that will help you name your wounds, build resilience, and grow through adversity. This isn't just self-care. It's soul care. And it's the missing piece for so many leaders today.

Here's what I know: The greatest gift you can give the people you lead is a healthy, whole you. When your soul is strong, your leadership is strong. When your heart is whole, your decisions are clear. When your inner world is healthy, your influence grows.

So don't just read this book—let it read you. Let it challenge you, encourage you, and guide you back to the kind of leader God created you to be: a leader who doesn't lead from pressure or performance but from wholeness.

I'm proud of Steve. I'm grateful to call him a friend. And I believe what he's written here will help you lead stronger and live healthier—from the inside out.

Your friend,
John C. Maxwell

Why I Wrote This Book

After thirty-five years in leadership, I've discovered a critical truth: Unhealed trauma doesn't just affect us personally—it influences how we impact others. This book emerged from three intersecting paths in my life.

First, my own personal trauma story gave me experience with the mental and emotional fragmentation trauma creates. I've walked through the journey of healing and witnessed the transformation possible when we address our own wounds.

Second, my decades of being a pastor, leader, coach, and mentor to other leaders have shown me the wreckage that occurs when leaders carry unprocessed trauma into their lives and roles. I've seen gifted individuals derail their calling because they never addressed the trauma and inner fragmentation of their souls.

Third, this book represents the culmination of three years of doctoral research under the mentoring of Dr. Tom Mullins, where I concentrated on the intersection of trauma and leadership. Additionally, I commissioned a leading research firm in a first-of-its-kind national study, *Leaders and Trauma Today*. We surveyed 750 US leaders across both for-profit and non-profit fields and gained new insights on how trauma impacts leaders. Together, this research and real-world experience have convinced me of this: Trauma doesn't need to have the final say in your life and leadership; you can heal, and even grow, on the other side of adversity.

Who This Book Is For

While this book is written *to* leaders, it's not *only for* leaders. The principles within apply to everyone. Whether you lead a multinational organization, pastor a church, manage a team, or simply want to understand how trauma affects your life and leadership, here you'll find practical pathways toward healing and wholeness.

It's important to note that I am writing as a leadership practitioner with an informed perspective, not as a licensed therapist or medical professional. The insights shared herein are not intended as medical advice or to replace professional mental health treatment. If you're struggling with trauma or mental health challenges, I encourage you to consult a physician and/or mental health professional today.

What's in This Book

The book unfolds in two main sections. In part 1, we ask the question: "What is going on with me?" We'll explore how trauma fragments your soul and leadership, causing you to lose your sense of well-being and straining your relationships with others. You'll understand the trauma-triggers effect and how unhealed wounds can resurface in high-pressured leadership moments.

In part 2, we ask: "Where do I go from here?" In this section, you'll discover a dual approach: preparing yourself for life's hardest moments while learning to heal when those moments leave their mark. Through the resilience equation, you'll increase your capacity for when crises inevitably come. We'll also explore the growth model to help you live and lead from wholeness through every challenge. Along the way, you'll find practical tools to build resilience and lead from a place of wholeness rather than trauma-induced fragmentation.

Trauma often leaves people feeling victimized. It's important to note victimhood is a disempowering state that leaves us feeling helpless. Your circumstances may have been unjust, deeply painful, and even shattering, yet you have the power to find healing and grow stronger through the pain. This book teaches you to take responsibility for your well-being and move beyond trauma's impact. My prayer is that these pages offer both hope and healing for your journey toward *shalom*[1]—the "wholeness" God intended for you from the beginning.

PART 1

WHAT IS GOING ON WITH ME?

CHAPTER 1

Soul Leadership

The sky outside loomed overcast and ominous, funnel clouds still swirling eerily overhead. A day after Hurricane Katrina's fury, strong winds continued to whip through the air as the atmosphere stirred in threatening transition. The air clung thick with moisture and tension as I stood next to several local police officers and fellow pastors, gathered to coordinate our efforts to help the region. We saw one another in the daylight that filtered through our church foyer windows. Our power was out, so it was the only place well-lit enough for us to meet.

"How can we help?" I asked.

The police chief answered, "Pastor, we really need to get fallen trees off of our officers' homes so I can get them to work. We need your help."

Dozens of faces of people who could assist ran through my head. "We can do that," I said.

Before I could say another word, our conversation was interrupted by a metallic pounding on our steel front door. Startled, I moved quickly, pulling it open to reveal a ten-year-old boy, his eyes wide and desperate. In his trembling hands, he clutched the oxygen tank he'd slammed against our door like a lifeline.

"Please," he gasped, his voice raw with panic. "My grandmother . . . she's dying! She needs oxygen . . . she needs help!"

His plea echoed in the foyer, piercing every heart in the room. At that moment, reality crashed down on me with brutal clarity: *If we don't do something, someone's going to die.* We sent help immediately to go with the young boy and care for his grandmother. In that moment, my responsibility wasn't just leadership theory I learned in a book; this was real life knocking at our door.

At thirty-six, my life was full. I had a young family, a rapidly growing church, and dreams unfolding faster than I'd ever imagined. But on August 29, 2005, Hurricane Katrina changed everything in one fierce blow. Due to the flooding and wind damage, more than one million people were displaced in southeast Louisiana and south Mississippi.[2] Our church in the New Orleans suburb of Mandeville went from a small group of nineteen people in 1999 to a large congregation of 3,200 attending on the weekend in less than six years. Katrina sliced our attendance to less than half overnight.

The leaders stood with me in stunned silence after the boy left. We were all grappling with a disaster the scope of which none of us had grasped. I broke the silence.

"Let's go and see what else we can do to help."

"I have a van and enough gas to get us into New Orleans," the police chief responded.

It was time to go to ground zero. We wound our way through broken-down cars and debris in what felt like a war zone. The city of New Orleans was underwater. We watched stranded people being rescued by boats from the roofs of their houses. We saw looters shatter windows with crowbars, breaking into abandoned stores and taking advantage of the tragedy. Dead bodies slumped on the overpass rails and lay crumpled beneath the underpasses close to the Superdome. The airport had turned into a medical triage center, people organized by the severity of their wounds along terminal gates.

The images of that day are burned into my memory.

All told, the storm covered 75 percent of New Orleans in water,[3] claimed 1,833 lives, and caused more than $125 billion in damages devastating our area.[4] I ran at full throttle on adrenaline for almost a year helping our region recover.

The Invisible Weight of Leading Through Crisis

In the grueling weeks that followed, a national leader suggested I get recovery efforts in motion and then consider moving to another city. He said, "There's no guarantee this won't happen again." Yet, I couldn't escape the young boy's pleading eyes or the countless faces of neighbors who'd lost everything. My wife and I didn't even consider leaving. We knew this was our city, our region, and our calling.

In the ensuing chaos—leading a team, coordinating thousands of volunteers, navigating crushing financial pressures—I moved as though underwater, sluggish, and heavy-limbed. After a year, I was completely drained. I struggled to meaningfully engage with my family while serving my community, never realizing the weight pressing against my chest had a name: *crisis-induced trauma*. I was drowning in it, though I didn't yet know the phrase

Trauma became a hallmark of Hurricane Katrina, even over a decade afterward.[5] Of the 1.2–1.5 million people evacuated, 62 percent met the criteria for acute stress disorder (ASD).[6]

And roughly one-third of New Orleans residents developed post-traumatic stress disorder (PTSD).[7] Peoples' internal devastation was as profound as the external destruction.

But here's the critical truth we'll explore together: It doesn't take a hurricane for someone to experience serious trauma. About 70 percent of US adults experience trauma at some point in their lives.[8] Shockingly, this number is even higher for leaders. Our study found that 93.7 percent of American leaders have experienced trauma, adversity, or periods of prolonged stress![9]

About 70 percent of US adults experience trauma at some point in their lives.

The fact is, leaders are in the trenches with people while also carrying heightened burdens and responsibilities. For me, the weight of leadership through Katrina—and subsequent events we'll discuss in this book—traumatized and fragmented my soul. So, if nine out of ten leaders experience trauma, adversity, or prolonged stress, it's worth asking these questions: What happens when trauma goes unprocessed? And, how does this impact your soul and leadership?

The truth is, *trauma doesn't self-resolve.* It doesn't stay compartmentalized. Psychological trauma affects our brains, souls, and even our bodies in dramatic ways most of us don't realize.[10] Psychological trauma is "any disturbing experience that results in significant fear, helplessness, dissociation, confusion, or other disruptive feelings intense enough to have a long-lasting negative effect on a person's attitudes, behavior, and other aspects of functioning."[11]

Studies have shown as much as 81 percent of mental health disorders are caused by trauma.[12] For leaders, this presents a profound risk not just for themselves but for everyone they influence. Unhealed trauma often wounds both those closest to us and those we lead. This means the larger a leader's influence, the greater the damage that can be done. The pain you carry doesn't just hurt you; it spills over onto others. Conversely, trauma experienced by a member of the leader's team can also traumatically affect the leader. Trauma is a two-way street.

The pain you carry doesn't just hurt you; it spills over onto others.

What Is Trauma?

Before we go further, let's be clear about what trauma looks like. Psychological trauma isn't the painful event itself. It's your brain's and body's response to a painful *crisis* or repeated *crises* determined by multiple factors. According to the American Psychological Association, a crisis is "a situation that produces significant cognitive or emotional stress in those involved in it."[13] Traumatic experiences can take many forms, including:

- physical or sexual abuse[14]
- neglect or abandonment[15]
- experiencing serious accidents or medical trauma[16]
- being subjected to bullying or harassment[17]
- encountering sudden loss of a loved one[18]
- living through a high-conflict divorce or custody battle[19]
- enduring betrayal by a trusted person or institution[20]

- experiencing or witnessing domestic violence or community violence[21]
- experiencing natural disasters like hurricanes or earthquakes[22]
- enduring chronic poverty[23]
- surviving war, terrorism, or displacement as a refugee[24]
- facing incarceration or the incarceration of a close family member[25]
- experiencing repeated exposure to trauma through caregiving, military service, or first responder roles[26]

Acute stress disorder (ASD) and post-traumatic stress disorder (PTSD) can result from sudden, intense events (like Hurricane Katrina) or the cumulative toll of prolonged stress, underscoring stress as the essential factor in traumatic experiences. From our research, three factors of traumatic crises stand out:

1. Duration: How long does the crisis last?
2. Frequency: How often do crises occur?
3. Intensity: How distressing was the crisis?

Perhaps that ten-year-old boy with an oxygen tank at your doorstep represents an unexpected crisis. For you, it could represent that trusted colleague who betrayed your confidence. Perhaps it is the marriage that dissolved into bitterness. Or, your child battling substance abuse. Maybe it's the unforeseen legal battle threatening everything you've built. Or, even those childhood wounds you've buried but never truly healed.

When traumatic experiences collide with leadership responsibilities, the weight becomes exponentially more difficult, even to the point of being unbearable. Yet many attempt to carry on without acknowledging the pain or seeking help for various reasons. As you guide your organization forward while taking on the hundreds of small and large burdens of leadership and extending yourself beyond reasonable limits, recognize that no one is immune to human pain and limitations. Even the most resilient among us has a breaking point, and acknowledging your vulnerability isn't weakness but wisdom. The truth about living in perpetual crisis is this: It's not a matter of *if* but *when* you will become traumatized.

When traumatic experiences collide with leadership responsibilities, the weight becomes exponentially more difficult, even to the point of being unbearable.

Leaders are particularly vulnerable to what is called *compounding trauma*.[27] It's the buildup of stressors that, individually, might be manageable but collectively overwhelm our normal coping mechanisms. The attending consequences can extend far beyond our own personal suffering, collaterally injuring families, communities, and organizations.

Psychological Trauma's Effect on the Brain

As a child, I remember riding in the car on a spring day and seeing an emergency room marked with big letters beneath it: Trauma Unit.

I asked my mom, "Why do people go there?"

"People go there because of car crashes, bad falls, gunshot wounds, and other accidents that really hurt them," she replied.

Often, these patients would be diagnosed with what is now known as traumatic brain injury (TBI). A TBI is caused by a blunt force that causes structural damage to the brain. Likewise, psychological trauma that occurs through prolonged stress, abuse, natural disasters, and the like doesn't just affect someone's mental state; it changes the physical brain as well.[28] This is a critical challenge for anyone who experiences psychological trauma.

The good news is the effects of psychological trauma can be temporary, and you can be healed.

In short, psychological trauma doesn't just impact how you feel; it actually changes your brain's structure and the way it functions. Ultimately, trauma causes *dis-integration* and fragmentation. This disruption weakens our leadership and leads to poor decision-making that hurts us and those we lead. A leader often becomes fragmented without realizing it. Unfortunately, I've had a front-row seat to many leaders who lived and led from this compromised place—and the results were disastrous.

The good news is the effects of psychological trauma can be temporary, and you can be healed. This healing journey requires an integrative approach to soul healing that we'll explore further throughout this book.

Soul Leadership: The Missing Ingredient

At the core of this book lies a transformative concept I call *soul leadership*, the essential foundation upon which all other leadership dimensions rest.

While self-leadership has gained well-deserved attention over the past decade as a pathway to personal wellness and responsibility, soul leadership represents something deeper and more fundamental. Soul leadership begins with an awareness of the health of your mind: your thoughts, will, and emotions. Most leaders are hard-driving and action-oriented, and the last thing they want to do is slow down and understand what's happening on the inside.

The conventional leadership progression is well-established: Self-leadership develops into team leadership, which evolves into organizational leadership. However, this framework can overlook a critical precursor: soul leadership, the inner foundation that makes authentic self-leadership possible.

Soul Leadership ▸ Self-Leadership ▸ Team Leadership ▸ Organizational Leadership ▸ Impact

Soul leadership contains the stewardship of your inner landscape—the state of wholeness or fragmentation that determines how you navigate your internal world. It's about the health of your core identity, foundational values, emotional patterns, and spiritual condition. These ultimately shape every aspect of your leadership impact.

The progression is clear and consequential: Healthy soul leadership creates the conditions for effective self-leadership. Effective self-leadership nurtures thriving teams. Thriving teams build excellent organizations. Excellent organizations maximize their positive impact in every sphere they touch.

Since trauma causes your brain to psychologically and physically *dis-integrate*, engaging in soul leadership is essential because it takes your mental and emotional states into account. The Bible says it this way: "Above all else, guard your heart, for everything you do flows from it" (Proverbs 4:23). The Old Testament was originally written in Hebrew. And the Hebrew word for "heart" means your inner self, will, understanding, or mind. Guarding your heart is the essence of soul leadership. Deeper than "self-care," it's "soul care."

In order to further explain soul leadership, we must understand the Hebrew concept of *shalom*—complete wholeness or integration. It's the idea behind the word *integrity* (from *integer*, meaning whole). The leadership crisis we see across the cultural landscape today—illustrated by rampant moral failures, ethical compromises, and destructive behaviors—is fundamentally a crisis of integrity or internal wholeness. Trauma is an enemy of wholeness. It restructures the brain and fragments the mind as the body responds to stress and crisis. When your soul is fragmented, which is what trauma does, everything you lead is at risk of being negatively impacted. It's difficult to create unity, connection, and healthy relationships in an organization when the soul of a leader lacks integration. The ultimate goal of soul leadership is precisely this: *wholeness*—moving from a state of fragmentation to one where leaders can live and lead from a place of authentic integration.

For example, I once knew a young leader named Paul. He was the kind of leader who lit up a room. With his quick smile, powerful speaking skills, and natural charm, he seemed destined for success.

On paper, Paul was the complete package. He could sell ice to penguins. When Paul talked about his vision, you couldn't help but want to be part of it.

Yet behind the charismatic front, Paul's organization was struggling with a persistent problem: No matter what he tried, his team never seemed to gel. The office atmosphere often felt tense. Conversations would stop when he entered a room. Projects that required collaboration frequently stalled or failed.

Most troubling was the revolving door of talent. In just a few years, Paul had replaced almost his entire staff—twice. Exit interviews revealed a pattern of complaints about unclear expectations, favoritism, and a culture where people felt undervalued.

"I don't understand what's happening," Paul confided to a friend. "I hire the best people. I pay well. Why can't I build a stable team?"

Determined to fix the problem, Paul invested heavily in external solutions. He hired prestigious consultants who conducted assessments and delivered recommendations. He brought in leadership coaches to help clarify values and build a healthy culture. The company handbook grew thick with mission statements, core values, and organizational expectations. Still, the problems persisted.

Paul doubled down on organizational fixes. More team-building exercises. More clarity on processes. More leadership books distributed to managers. Yet with each new initiative, the workplace culture remained toxic, and the turnover continued unabated.

What Paul never recognized was that the instability he witnessed throughout his organization originated not from his team or his strategies but from within his own soul. The toxicity wasn't coming from his organization; it was flowing from his own unresolved internal pain and unprocessed traumas.

Today, Paul's company remains a shell of what he had envisioned—fledgling at best. The pattern continues as he moves from one organizational solution to another, never addressing the fundamental truth: The fragmentation he sees around him is merely reflecting the fragmentation in his own life.

Paul's story serves as a powerful reminder that organizations inevitably mirror their leaders—through what psychologists have identified as "mirror neurons" (that we'll discuss in the next chapter). No amount of external consulting or team development can overcome the limitations of a leader who fails to do the hard work of personal growth. In the end, Paul created an impressive vision for everyone else's development but never seemed to include himself in that process.

The First Trauma

To understand trauma's impact on leadership, we must examine humanity's original wholeness and what fractured it. Trauma is among our oldest human experiences. At creation, God called everything "very good" (Genesis 1:31), a state of completion and *shalom* (wholeness). Adam and Eve existed in perfect harmony with God, each other, and creation. Every need was met.

Think about when you feel most alive in life and work. Isn't it when you have physical comfort, safety, meaningful connections, recognition, and a sense of purpose? This integration of needs reflects our original design for wholeness.[29]

While Abraham Maslow's Hierarchy of Needs[30] (physiological, security, belonging, esteem, and self-actualization) provides a useful framework, I believe complete wholeness only emerges through relationship with God. The garden of Eden represented this perfection—all physical needs satisfied, complete safety, divine community, inherent value, and meaningful purpose.

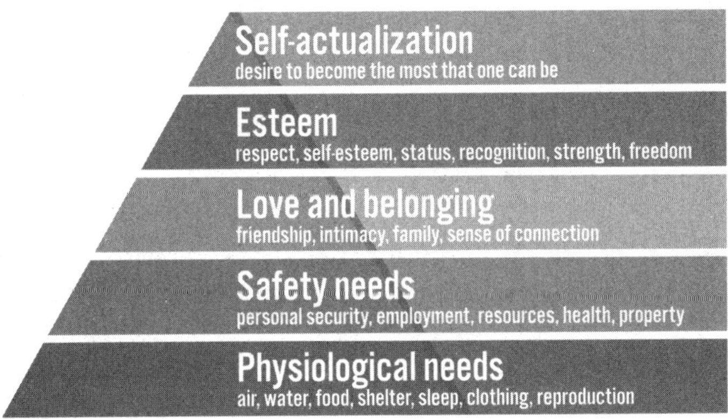

Yet this wholeness shattered when trust broke. When Adam and Eve disobeyed God, sin fractured the entire created order. The effects were immediate and comprehensive:

- **Physiological needs:** The ground was cursed, making it harder to harvest food.
- **Safety needs:** Their sense of safety was shattered as they hid from God in fear, a condition that intensified dramatically after Cain murdered Abel (Genesis 4).
- **Love and belonging:** Adam and Eve's connection with God and each other fractured.

- **Esteem:** Adam blaming Eve showed her that she had lost value in her husband's eyes (Genesis 3:12).
- **Self-actualization (purpose):** Instead of working on their mission as image bearers, they struggled to meet daily needs.

What was once integrated became fragmented. Wholeness gave way to brokenness. This original crisis introduced trauma into human existence, and its effects have torn through leadership ever since.

The Stress Continuum: From Stress to Trauma

To understand the crises that cause trauma, we need to grasp the primary force: stress. The stress I'm talking about is not a singular state but a continuum that progresses from healthy pressure to debilitating chronic stress (as Adam, Eve, and the rest of humanity have experienced from the beginning).

The Stress Continuum

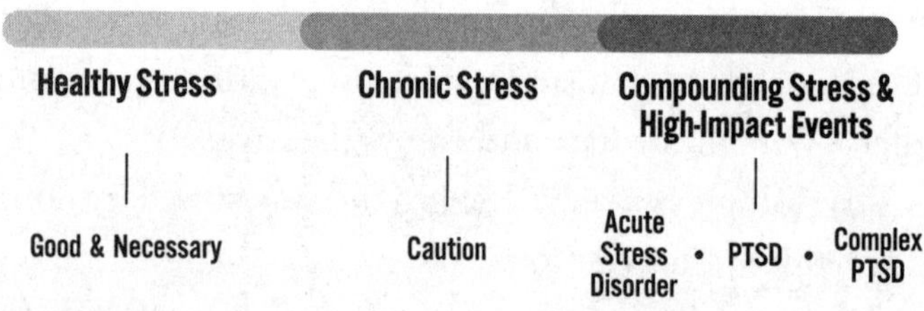

Visually, we can think of stress as a spectrum with three distinct zones:

- **Healthy Stress:** The good stress, called "eustress,"[31] promotes growth and development—like muscles strengthening after exercise. This stress challenges us but remains within our capacity to recover and grow.[32]
- **Chronic Stress:** The cautionary stage where damage begins to accumulate. According to researchers at Yale Medicine, "Chronic stress slowly drains a person's psychological resources and damages their brains and bodies."[33] This is where burnout emerges.
- **Traumatic Stress:** When stress overwhelms our ability to cope, due to crises that can lead to psychological trauma and the *dis-integration* of the brain.

When leaders remain in the chronic stress and compounding stress zones too long, the structure of our brains literally changes.

When leaders remain in the chronic stress and compounding stress zones too long, the structure of our brains literally changes. Prolonged stress reshapes parts of the brain that handle emotions, stress responses, planning, decision-making, and memory. This particularly affects the prefrontal cortex (responsible for executive function) and the amygdala (the emotional center). These changes cause both structural and functional problems.[34]

Think of it like Hurricane Katrina. The state of your post-trauma brain is like the Gulf Coast after Hurricane Katrina hit and before relief efforts had begun.

The Cascading Effects of Unprocessed Trauma

I'll never forget the call I received years ago. "Steve, I'm not doing well," the pastor's voice trembled on the other end of the line. "I'm in a dark hole, and I can't get out. I really need some help."

My heart sank. I knew what John had been through. A difficult building campaign had drained both resources and morale. Personal challenges had mounted at home. Staffing issues created constant fires to extinguish. The pressures of leading an expanding organization while balancing life's demands had become overwhelming.

A chief peril of leadership isn't simply incompetence or even weariness–it's unprocessed trauma.

It wasn't one crisis that broke John. It was the endless barrage of compounding, trauma-inducing events. He had finally reached his breaking point, and he was calling for help.

To this day, I regret not getting on a plane and showing up at John's house. A struggling leader needs more than distant advice. They need someone physically present in their darkest hour. My friend was suffering what many leaders face: unhealed trauma rearing its ugly head. You see, a chief peril of leadership isn't simply incompetence or even weariness—it's unprocessed trauma.

When leaders carry traumatic wounds they haven't addressed, these wounds affect their decisions, relationships, and organizational cultures. The cascading effects can be devastating:

- Decision-making becomes compromised as trauma triggers hypervigilance or avoidance.[35]

- Emotional intelligence breaks down as trauma disrupts self-awareness, regulation, and empathy.[36]
- Relationships suffer as unprocessed pain creates defensive patterns and unhealthy coping strategies.[37]
- Organizational culture can deteriorate as the leader's fragmented internal state reproduces itself throughout the entire organization.

Today, leaders frequently make headlines for failures, indiscretions, moral corruption, and abuses of power. When we examine the backstories of these fallen leaders, unprocessed psychological traumas often emerge as root causes of the behaviors that eventually brought them down.

When we examine the backstories of these fallen leaders, unprocessed psychological traumas often emerge as root causes of the behaviors that eventually brought them down.

According to a Barna Group study, "Trauma is rarely a one-time occurrence."[38] Instead, it compounds. Prior trauma creates vulnerability to further trauma and is a strong predictor of developing severe stress responses to crises like PTSD. This sets off a dangerous cycle of harm for those in leadership positions.[39]

The Soul Leadership Cycle: Your Path to Resilience

Based on extensive research, real leadership stories, historical examples, and current science, I developed what I call the soul-leadership cycle. Though not perfectly linear, it has three parts:

The Trauma-Triggers Effect	The Resilience Equation	The Growth Model

1. **The Trauma-Triggers Effect:** This effect shows how unhealed trauma can suddenly resurface during high-pressure leadership moments and negatively affect our behavior. Understanding this concept helps us manage those moments. (Chapter 5)
2. **The Resilience Equation:** Resilience is the key to handling crises. The good news is that everyone can build their resilience—the ability to absorb and rebound from adversity—by increasing capacity before a crisis hits and even afterward. (Chapters 6–8)
3. **The Growth Model:** This model shows how leaders can recover from, and even grow after, painful experiences. The opportunity to grow emotionally, psychologically, and spiritually is inherent in all of our crisis responses. The growth model also highlights neuroplasticity—the brain's ability to rewire itself—and demonstrates how you can emerge stronger after healing from trauma. (Chapters 9–10)

Three Truths About the Healing Journey

Here's what I've learned in my journey through trauma and healing. First, as a leader who's personally navigated this journey, I understand the isolation and complexity of the process. The path to wholeness can feel impossible, but I assure you it's not. Second, mental resilience can be developed both preventively (before crisis) and restoratively (after trauma occurs). You can learn to increase capacity that protects you and those you lead. The pathway to resilience isn't just about enduring hardship. It's the dual capacity to absorb difficult experiences and to bounce back from them. Third, trauma doesn't have to be the end of your story. What psychologists call "post-traumatic growth"—not just surviving trauma but emerging stronger—is possible for every person who commits to the journey of processing in a healthy way.

For our purposes, we'll define a leader as someone who assumes responsibility for another. With this definition, the stakes become clear: Leaders either help heal or unintentionally transmit their traumatic wounds to those they lead.

People need to feel safe. It's how we're wired. When we feel safe, we trust others, especially those who lead us. Trust makes leadership work, and it comes naturally from leaders who live with the kind of wholeness God designed us for. When leaders take time to heal and do their own work, they create spaces for others to do the same. Leaders who don't address their own pain often pass that hurt on to others, sometimes without even knowing it.

Your Path to Wholeness

I'm drawn back to that day after Katrina when the young man with the oxygen tank banged on our church building door. That moment crystallized the weight of leadership that comes as a result of crisis. In those situations, our decisions carry heavy consequences for both ourselves and those we lead.

God's call and mandate for leadership go all the way back to Genesis 2:15, when he instructed Adam to "work . . . and take care of" the garden. This speaks of stewarding well what's been entrusted to our care—including people.

Interestingly, the Hebrew word used for "guard" in Proverbs 4:23 is similar to the word used in Genesis 2:15. These principles are parallel. Soul leadership is the seedbed and strength behind your leadership influence. If you're not tending your inner self well, it will manifest in how you steward and lead your organization. A damaged soul in a leader has the potential to damage an entire organization. As the adage says, "*Hurt* people, hurt people." The cracks in our inner world eventually spread to everything we touch.

So, leader to leader, I ask you an important question: How is your soul?

A damaged soul in a leader has the potential to damage an entire organization.

Don't rush past this question. Your honest answer predicts your future if nothing changes. If you're thriving with healthy rhythms, capacity, and resilience, that's wonderful. This book will help inform you through others' challenges, deepen resilience practices, and increase your sustainability and leadership impact. If, however, you're exhausted, battling psychological trauma, easily triggered, or have left a wake of broken relationships, know there is hope. A path to healing, increased resilience, and longevity is available to you.

In the next chapter, we explore how the brain and mind work together—an understanding that will help you become a better leader. This book isn't just about personal growth; it's about helping you build thriving organizations that make lasting impacts. As you apply these principles, you will be practicing soul leadership to produce excellence in both your life and leadership. The roadblocks that once limited your effectiveness will become launching pads for unprecedented growth. Your leadership can produce something significant, creating vibrant teams, breakthrough innovations, and organizational cultures where people thrive. The journey to *shalom* starts with unveiling the mystery of how your brain and soul work together. Get ready to become the extraordinary leader you've always desired to be.

CHAPTER 2

Our Fragmented Minds

Imagine your brain and mind like a sophisticated computer system. Your brain represents the hardware—the distinct physical components that work in harmony when functioning properly. Your mind serves as the software—your operating system. This is who you are. It's your essential being where information is processed, values and meaning are formed, and moral judgments are made. The brain is very intricate and complex. In the simplest terms, the parts of the brain most impacted by stress and crisis are the limbic system and the prefrontal cortex.

The brain constantly adjusts to environmental changes to maintain stability.[40] When conditions shift, the brain adapts to keep its parts working together properly. To understand how emotional events and ongoing stress affect us, we need to see how different brain regions respond.

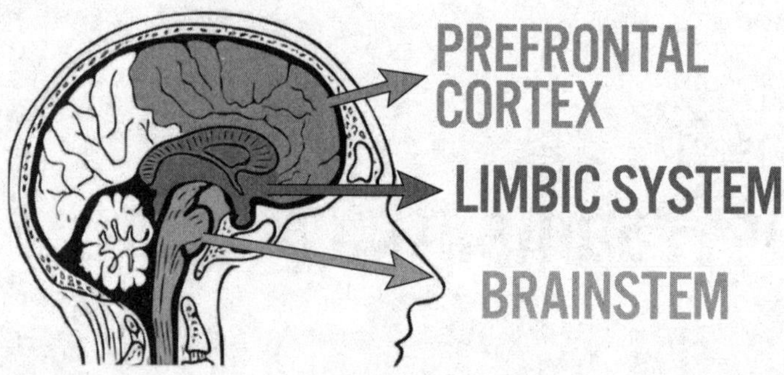

- **The brainstem** (bottom section) handles basic body functions like breathing, heart rate, temperature, and pain sensing. It makes sure all your bodily systems work correctly.
- **The limbic system** (middle section) is a group of interrelated parts of the brain like the amygdala and hippocampus that help process emotions, produce instincts, trigger behaviors, and store memories as images, sensations, and feelings.[41]
- **The prefrontal cortex** (top section) coordinates with other parts of the brain for higher mental functions such as thinking, speaking, reasoning, and logical processing.

Your brain is incredibly complex and powerful. Day and night, even while you sleep, it's busy processing information.[42] Billions of tiny nerve cells called neurons constantly send messages back and forth throughout your entire brain, creating a massive communication network where messages travel at lightning speed.[43]

In a healthy state, your brain works efficiently, sorting through all incoming information and deciding where to send each message. It follows familiar patterns when life runs smoothly, with all parts working together in harmony—integrated and interdependent. Yet, under extreme stress and crisis, the brain can malfunction.

The Blob Effect

Over the years I've taken each of my four children to an adventure camp in Northern California. One of our favorite activities was "the blob" on the lake. It's a giant inflatable pillow floating on the water where one person sits on the far end while another jumps from a platform onto the near end. The force of the jump compressing one end sends a wave of air through the blob, lifting the other end, and launching the person into the air and down into the water. You can't isolate the impact as the entire blob responds as one connected system. Press down on one spot and the force travels through every part of it, ultimately catapulting someone skyward. The energy doesn't disappear or stay put: It moves and reshapes the blob, transforming one person's downward force into another's upward flight.

This water blob analogy is similar to how trauma affects our brains. When we experience traumatic events or prolonged stress, our brains don't break into disconnected pieces. Instead, like that blob, the pressure of traumatic experiences causes a restructuring. The normal communications between parts of our brains become interrupted, and the brain's ability to process information in a healthy manner is compromised.[44]

In response to overwhelming stress, some parts of our brains become hyperactive—constantly vigilant, scanning for danger, easily startled—while other parts, like our ability to focus on simple tasks or remember conversations, seem to shrink. The amygdala, our brain's alarm system housed in the limbic system, starts taking up more "space" in our mental functioning. At the same time, the prefrontal cortex, responsible for logical thinking, gets pushed down like the near end of that water blob.[45]

This is why people often have unexpected emotional reactions after trauma. They become what's often called "easily triggered" or "activated." It's not that the brain has physically separated but rather it has restructured itself in response to trauma, becoming *dis-integrated.* Information from the crisis remains unprocessed and improperly stored—like a "clog" in the brain. This clog gets stuck in the limbic system, where emotions and memories are handled, creating ongoing disruption in how the brain functions as a whole.

Both your internal mental state and environmental factors influence your brain's ability to function in a healthy way. When trauma disrupts our brain's natural integration, the good news is that just like a water blob can return back to its original form, our brains can regain healthy equilibrium. The scientific community refers to this state as *homeostasis.* The brain is neuroplastic, which means after periods of extreme stress, it has the amazing capacity to realign, reconnect, and reorganize back to health.[46] Think of it like trails in a forest. The paths you walk most often become clearer and easier to travel. Similarly, when brain cells fire together repeatedly, they create stronger connections.

Understanding this integrated view of brain function and how extreme stress and trauma affect it helps us be more patient with the healing process. Recovery involves helping the brain restore its natural state of integration, where all parts—brainstem, limbic system, prefrontal cortex, and the rest—can once again work together harmoniously, adapting to life's changes while maintaining stability and proper function.

Unlike the water blob that returns to its original form on its own, our brains require help to return to homeostasis. By intentionally processing trauma we enable our brains to rewire in a healthy way. If our brains—the hardware—can be restructured, then our minds—the software—can be renewed. Before we press on, it's helpful to ask: What is the mind?

If our brains–the hardware–can be restructured, then our minds–the software–can be renewed.

Revealing the Mystery of the Mind

Typically, *mind* and *soul* are used synonymously, both describing the same reality of our inner world. In the Bible, we see this connection when the apostle Paul described humans as three-part beings consisting of "spirit, soul and body" (1 Thessalonians 5:23). The mind (or soul) is indelibly tied to our will and emotions. It's not merely a collection of thoughts; it's the framework, the lens, the grid through which we see and interpret the world around us.

Unlike the brain, which functions as the physical control center for our nervous system, the mind involves our thoughts and beliefs, and shapes our perspective on reality. Though

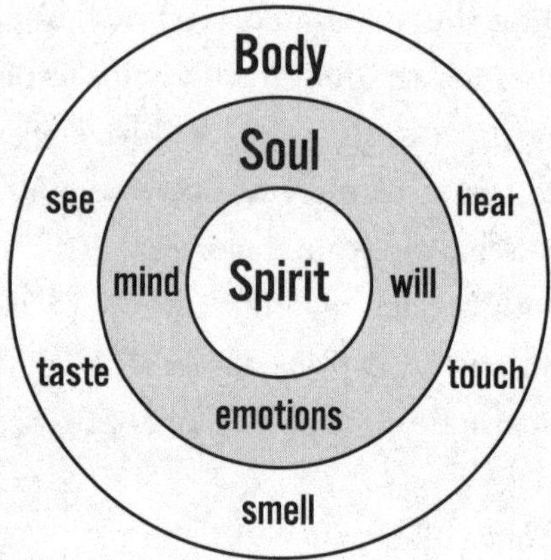

distinct, the mind and brain are so closely connected they're like a duplex with one front door.

What Scripture declared thousands of years ago, science now confirms: "For as he thinks in his heart, so is he" (Proverbs 23:7 NKJV). Our thoughts are not merely fleeting ideas but measurable realities that actively create physical "real estate" in our brains. Every thought influences our decisions, words, actions, and even our physical reactions.

In my twenties, I started an organization that helped junior high and high school students make positive life choices. During my years speaking to them, I loved using a lemon demonstration to show how our thoughts affect us. I would ask everyone to close their eyes and imagine holding a lemon and cutting it open. Then in a loud and playful tone I would say, "Now lick the lemon!" Almost every time, you could hear gasps around the room as kids physically reacted to just imagining that sourness. Their minds (thoughts) created a physiological response in their bodies. This powerful mind-body connection illustrates why renewing our minds is critical.

Understanding the power of the mind-body connection gives us great insight into Paul's words he wrote in Romans, "Do not conform to the pattern of this world, but be transformed by the renewing of your mind" (12:2). Being conformed to the world is when our thoughts and actions reflect our selfish tendencies, ideologies, and philosophies. Being transformed means changing the way we think—our thoughts, emotions, and attitudes. Paul used the Greek word *metamorphoō*, from which we get "metamorphosis." Just as a caterpillar transforms into a butterfly, our minds can undergo radical change through the power of God's Word. This transformation takes us from weakness to strength, from fragmentation to wholeness.

Practically speaking, renewing our mind follows a three-step process:

1. Taking responsibility for our thoughts
2. Rejecting unhealthy and toxic mindsets
3. Rescripting our minds by speaking and meditating on God's truth

When trauma affects the brain, the brain gets restructured, but it also impacts the mind and soul, creating fractures. The beauty lies in how science and faith come together for personal wholeness. As we replace misbeliefs with God's truth, we shift from the classic "stinking thinking" to a mind that reflects a healthy perspective. This renewal transforms our thoughts, emotions, choices, habits, character, and ultimately, our destiny.

Thoughts ▸ Emotions ▸ Choices ▸ Habits ▸ Character ▸ Destiny

This is the miracle of neuroplasticity, our brain's capacity to be rewired, viewed through a spiritual lens. As our brains realign, our minds can be renewed through the life-changing power of God's Word. God designed us this way.

Your Brain and Mind in Soul Leadership

When we examine the foundation of soul leadership, we must begin where leadership itself starts, inside a leader's integrated or fragmented neural architecture. Your leadership health is proportional to your brain's integration and your mind's renewal. This isn't metaphorical—it's a biological reality.

Recall our water blob analogy. The pressure points created by trauma don't just affect isolated areas of your brain; they affect your body and can reshape your entire leadership paradigm. When your limbic system becomes hyperactive through chronic stress or crisis, your prefrontal cortex—responsible for strategic thinking, complex analysis, and ethical decision-making—becomes compromised. This neural restructuring inevitably manifests in your leadership behavior.

Consider what happened with Paul, the charismatic leader we discussed earlier. His revolving door of talent wasn't just an organizational issue—it was a neurobiological one. The fragmentation in his brain—likely caused by unprocessed childhood wounds and compounding leadership stressors—created *dis-integration* between his limbic system (emotional center) and prefrontal cortex (rational center). This neural dysregulation caused him to misread social cues, overreact to perceived threats, and fail to establish the emotional climate necessary for team cohesion and safety.

The brain regions most affected by stress and crisis play a critical role in your leadership effectiveness. All parts of the brain are foundational to sustainable leadership. Your limbic system governs emotional intelligence, relational connection, and value formation. This is the heart of authentic leadership. When trauma overwhelms the limbic system, leaders can become emotionally unavailable or volatile, negatively impacting psychological and relational safety within their organizations.

Your prefrontal cortex facilitates strategic thinking, moral reasoning, and purposeful action. Each of these inform your decision-making and vision-casting elements of leadership. Trauma-induced prefrontal impact can lead to shortsighted decisions, ethical compromises, and mission drift.[47]

This is why unprocessed traumatic experiences are particularly devastating for leaders. Crisis creates a neurobiological vulnerability that compounds with each additional stressor. This is especially true for leaders who've experienced childhood trauma. Most leaders experienced trauma before they stepped into their leadership role.[48] When adults who have experienced childhood trauma face new trauma-inducing events, they can develop unique problems that need attention. In fact, as mentioned earlier, early trauma can create patterns that make someone more vulnerable to trauma later in life.[49]

Childhood trauma, also known as developmental trauma,[50] can affect both the physical and emotional development of a person and can lead to adult psychoses. Research has documented abnormalities in the frontal lobe in adults of children who suffered abuse.[51] This is aggravated by what researcher Judith Herman called "Complex PTSD," a distinct condition resulting from prolonged early-life trauma.[52] This condition manifests in two main symptom clusters: intrusion symptoms[53] (such as nightmares and being constantly on high alert) and constriction symptoms (such as depression and social withdrawal). People with complex PTSD typically swing unpredictably between these two states, creating significant inner turmoil. This neurobiological dysregulation makes it extremely difficult to maintain stable relationships, as the person alternates between heightened reactivity and emotional numbness, often confusing and overwhelming those around them. When childhood trauma is blended with adult leadership trauma, the effects can be debilitating.

I experienced childhood difficulties myself. My biological father was an alcoholic, which led to a broken home life. My parents ended up divorcing when I was five years old. Growing up in West Des Moines, Iowa, I was the only child in kindergarten with divorced parents. My mother remarried, and they too experienced marriage difficulty for many years. By the time I was a teenager, I was often put in the position to play referee for my mother and stepfather's arguments. Thus, I began a strategy of trying to control my environment to gain internal peace. Though there were a number of rough years, thank God there's been healing in my family, and I've enjoyed a great relationship with my mom and stepfather throughout my adult life.

My difficult childhood experiences compounded, making me more vulnerable to trauma later in life. In a similar way, when I experienced the chaos of Hurricane Katrina during our growing church's sixth year, the tremendous stress caused extreme trauma in my brain. For a full year after Katrina, I lived in a constant state of high alert. Through years of research and counseling, I now understand what was happening: My emotional brain periodically took over my rational thinking. This hurt my leadership—not because I lacked knowledge or skills, but because my stressed brain affected my decisions, which impacted my family and those I was leading.

What makes this particularly dangerous is how a leader's neural fragmentation cascades throughout the organization.[54] Neurobiological research has identified "mirror neurons" that cause our brains to sync with those around us.[55] When a leader operates from a fragmented neural state, team members may unconsciously mirror this fragmentation. The leader's dysregulated nervous system can become the organization's dysregulated nervous system. Calm, integrated leaders create calm, integrated organizations. Calm, integrated parents create calm, integrated families. Fragmented, reactive leaders create fragmented, reactive organizations.

The warning signs of a traumatized leader are clear:

- Emotional volatility that creates walking-on-eggshells cultures
- Impulsive decision-making without adequate consultation
- Rigid thinking that resists adaptation
- Relational withdrawal that creates information silos
- Defensive responses to constructive feedback
- Increasingly centralized control to manage anxiety

These aren't just leadership style issues; they're symptoms of a brain in survival mode rather than integration mode. When leaders blame organizational dysfunction on external factors while ignoring their own brain and mind fragmentation, they miss the root cause. Practically, here's what this can look like in real life.

Greg's Story: Neural Fragmentation in Leadership

My friend Greg grew up surrounded by fear and chaos. As a child, he often stood between his fighting parents and saw terrible betrayal and violence. These traumatic experiences restructured his developing brain and terrorized his soul. His fear center became overactive while the thinking and decision-making part of his brain was hindered in development. To survive the chaos, his brain learned to disconnect his feelings from events. Psychologists call this depersonalization, which is a dissociative symptom in which a person feels detached from their own self (disconnected from their own thoughts, memories, feelings, surroundings, behavior, and identity).[56] This helped him endure painful experiences as a child, but later made it difficult for him to connect emotionally with those he led.

At seventeen, Greg received Christ, which gave his broken life an anchor. For the next ten years, he traveled as a speaker at youth events, finding stability and purpose. During this time, his brain began to heal through positive experiences and healthy relationships, though the old trauma pathways remained.

When Greg started a church that grew quickly, new problems emerged. Leadership, staff, and personal challenges activated his childhood wounds. Under this pressure his brain fell back into old survival patterns, at times making decisions based on fear rather than wisdom. As a survival mechanism, he would detach from situations because of the leadership pain, which at times made him seem aloof and disinterested in the needs of others. He would shut down emotionally, which resulted in people in his organization feeling he was harsh and lacking empathy.

The good news is that Greg found healing. He bravely stepped away from his prominent leadership position temporarily to focus on getting healthier. Through therapy and spiritual growth, he allowed his brain to rewire and pursued healthier mindsets before returning to lead. When he came back, it took a year to find his leadership footing. However, as he began to prioritize soul health, it created a thriving culture in his entire organization, showing how soul leadership works: Healthy leaders create healthy organizations.

Mind Renewal: The Pathway to Integrated Soul Leadership

If neural fragmentation creates dysregulated leadership, then mind renewal creates integrated soul leadership. This transformation doesn't happen automatically. It requires intentional restructuring of the brain (hardware) and renewing of the mind (software). A three-step process takes on profound significance for soul leadership.

Step One: Recognize Negative Mindsets and Take Ownership

Cultivating awareness of negative mindsets and taking ownership is the first step toward brain healing. There's a neuroscientific principle called Hebbian learning that says "neurons that fire together, wire together," which means your repeated thoughts actually create physical pathways in your brain.[57] The key is recognizing that harmful leadership patterns are just pathways in your brain, not permanent realities. When you take responsibility for your thought patterns, you activate your brain's command center, starting the corrective and healing process.

Step Two: Reject Toxic Thoughts

After recognizing harmful thought patterns, you need to actively work on removing them. The apostle Paul called this "to put off your old self" (Ephesians 4:22). You must identify the specific beliefs traumatic events created like *I must control everything to feel safe* or *Showing vulnerability is dangerous.* These thoughts form well-traveled neural pathways in your brain. To weaken these connections, you must consistently reject these beliefs after becoming aware of them.

Step Three: Rescript Your Leadership Perspective

As you challenge and reject harmful thought patterns, it's essential to build new, healthy ones to replace them. By focusing on truth and speaking life-giving thoughts aloud, you engage mental processes like reasoning and motivation, forming new commitments and intentions.[58] This practice, called positive self-talk, not only reinforces affirming beliefs but also helps rewire your brain, promoting lasting mental and emotional health. When you regularly think and talk about healthy leadership principles like serving others, being honest, showing compassion, pursuing excellence, and being a good steward, you're actually building new physical connections in your

Your neural pathways become your leadership highways.

brain. With time and practice, these new connections become your natural way of thinking and leading.

Your leadership isn't shaped by your external circumstances as much as it's shaped by your internal thoughts. Your neural pathways become your leadership highways. Leaders who constantly worry create anxious organizations. Leaders who see possibilities create thriving organizations.

This is why soul leadership must come first, before leading your team or your organization. If your brain isn't healthy and integrated, every other part of your leadership will suffer. Yet when your inner world is whole, all aspects of your leadership can flourish.

CHAPTER 3

The Tragedy of a Traumatized Leader

In 1945, twenty-seven-year-old Billy Graham emerged seemingly from nowhere to fill auditoriums across America, speaking to as many as thirty thousand people a night. His reputation as a uniquely gifted preacher spread across the US like wildfire. The rest, as they say, is history.

You've likely heard of Billy Graham, the greatest evangelist of the twentieth century. But have you ever heard of Bron Clifford? His name has largely been forgotten by history, yet his beginning was just as promising as Graham's—if not more so.[59]

Bron Clifford was a twenty-five-year-old spiritual fireball. In 1945, many believed Clifford was the most gifted and powerful preacher the church had seen in centuries. That year, when Clifford preached to an auditorium of thousands in Miami, Florida, people lined up outside, desperate to get in. Later that same year at Baylor University, the president of the school ordered class bells turned off so that the young man could preach without interruption. For two hours and fifteen minutes, he held students spellbound as he preached.

At just twenty-five, young Clifford touched more lives, influenced more leaders, and set more attendance records than any other clergyman his age in American history.[60] National leaders competed for his attention. He was tall, handsome, intelligent, and eloquent. Clifford was even invited to audition for a blockbuster Hollywood film. It seemed he had everything.

Both Graham and Clifford came shooting out of the starting blocks like missiles. Yet just nine years later, Clifford had lost his family, his ministry, his health, and then, tragically, his life. Alcohol and financial irresponsibility destroyed him. He abandoned his wife and their two children, who both had Down syndrome. His final job was selling used cars in the Texas Panhandle. Then, at just thirty-five years old, this once-great preacher died from cirrhosis of the liver in a run-down motel on the outskirts of Amarillo.

He died, as John Haggai put it, "unwept, unhonored, and unsung."[61] Local pastors in Amarillo collected money among themselves just to purchase a casket so his body could be shipped back East for burial in a cemetery for the poor.

In 1945, two young men with extraordinary gifts were preaching the gospel to thousands across the nation. Within ten years, only one remained faithful to his calling. What happened to Bron Clifford? How could someone with such promise fall so spectacularly?

Looking at Clifford's dramatic downfall, we can only wonder what painful experiences might have shaped him. What childhood wounds did he carry? Perhaps there were deep father issues that created unhealthy patterns in his life he tried to cover up with religious activity and success. When the pressure of his ministry grew too intense, it seems his religious facade became part of his problem rather than his solution. Unable to face his inner pain directly, he turned to negative coping strategies, including alcohol abuse, for temporary relief. This ultimately destroyed him.

His story bears striking parallels to that of King Saul in the Bible—a man anointed and gifted by God, tall and handsome, with every natural advantage, who ultimately self-destructed. Like Clifford, Saul catapulted to success as a young man. Their unprocessed psychological pain and the weight of success led to both men's eventual demise.

Shame, Fear, and Control

As I noted in chapter 1, psychological trauma is any deeply disturbing experience that causes intense fear or helplessness powerful enough to negatively affect a person's life long after the event has passed. It occurs when someone's inner being—their soul—experiences either a sudden crisis or endures prolonged stressful conditions that overwhelm their capacity to cope. The Bible contains many narratives of leaders with wounded, traumatized souls.

King Saul is a perfect example of how trauma can damage a leader. His story shows us what happens when a leader's soul becomes fragmented and healing doesn't take place.[62] Saul's story in 1 Samuel shows a man with great leadership abilities who accomplished significant political and military achievements, yet ended tragically. Throughout, we see signs that Saul suffered from psychological trauma rooted in shame, fear, and control. Leading from this wounded place, Saul nearly destroyed his family, government, and nation.

Saul's story began alongside the prophet Samuel. In 1 Samuel 9, we meet Saul, a handsome young man from the tribe of Benjamin. While searching for his father's lost donkeys, he encountered Samuel, who told him he would become king. Saul's response to this honor revealed a fragmented self-image: "Saul answered, 'But am I not a Benjamite, from the smallest tribe of Israel, and is not my clan the least of all the clans of the tribe of Benjamin? Why do you say such a thing to me?'" (1 Samuel 9:21).

At Saul's official coronation, another red flag appeared. They found him hiding behind the luggage and had to bring him out to crown him (1 Samuel 10:22–23). Samuel tried to build Saul up to the people, saying, "Do you see the man the LORD has chosen? There is no one like him among all the people" (1 Samuel 10:24). Yet some Israelites refused to accept Saul as their king (1 Samuel 10:27). In this way, Saul's deepest fear—*rejection*—came true, at least with some people. Three likely sources of Saul's shame are:

1. His tribal background
2. His family lineage
3. His father wounds

Saul's Tribal Background

When Saul put himself down about being from Benjamin, it wasn't just personal insecurity. It was rooted in a terrible historical event.

Decades before Saul, an Israelite from the tribe of Levi was traveling through Benjamin's territory and stopped in Saul's hometown of Gibeah for the night. A citizen of Gibeah offered him a place to stay. That night, men from Gibeah tried to sexually assault the Levite. Instead, they took his servant girl and assaulted her until she died. Word spread throughout Israel of this shameful atrocity. The other eleven tribes wanted to punish these men, but the tribe of Benjamin refused to turn them over. As a result, the eleven tribes attacked and crushed the entire tribe of Benjamin (Judges 19–20).

This shame and disgrace hung over the Benjamites for generations. Psychologists call this type of negative familial impact on Saul's soul "intergenerational transmission" of trauma.[63] Some people alive during Saul's time might even have lived through those awful events. First Samuel 9 shows us that Saul carried this tribal shame and lived in fear of being rejected because of it. Again, this is why Saul responded to the call to be king, saying, "But I'm from the smallest tribe in Israel and my clan is the least important!"

This tragedy reveals Saul's hidden struggle—a man haunted by shame and terrified of rejection. Have you ever noticed how many leaders reach the peak of success only to self-destruct? Behind those public failures often lies unaddressed shame. Perhaps it was childhood criticism, family trauma, or teenage humiliation they never processed.

The painful truth: Success doesn't heal shame; it often amplifies it. Here's the hope: God sees through our carefully constructed facades. He wants to heal those wounded places we've hidden away. Our greatest vulnerability might become our greatest strength—if we'll finally bring it into the light.

Saul's Forbidden Family Lineage

Scripture gives us an interesting clue about another source of Saul's shame: his unusual height. He's described as "a head taller than anyone else" (1 Samuel 9:2). This might seem like a compliment, but it actually points to something potentially troubling.

In Israel's history, this kind of description wasn't used for Israelites. It was used for Canaanites, people the Israelites had once described as frightening giants. One account tells how they felt like "grasshoppers" next to them (Numbers 13:32 MSG).

Saul's remarkable height suggests he might have had Canaanite ancestry, perhaps through a forbidden marriage between an Israelite father and a Canaanite mother. This would have been a significant source of shame, as God had specifically prohibited these marriages (Deuteronomy 7:3–4).

Imagine carrying that kind of secret shame while being thrust into national leadership. It helps explain why Saul struggled so deeply with belonging and acceptance. Maybe something similar is true for you?

Perhaps your parents made choices around your birth and upbringing that have impacted you to this day. My biological father was an orphan. Throughout his whole life, the feeling of abandonment stuck with him. Unless these wounds are healed, they can cause massive insecurities. That was Saul's story. Many people struggle with this shame and yet hold influential leadership positions. Oftentimes people seek out leadership positions to compensate for childhood feelings of inadequacy. Yet success does not quiet the voice of shame. You must be healed from that hurt.

Saul's Father Wounds

A careful examination of Saul's relationship with his father suggests Saul possibly carried deep-seated father wounds. In

1 Samuel 9, when Saul's father, Kish, sent him to find missing donkeys, he didn't send Saul off alone. For a grown man, this simple task shouldn't have required supervision. Could it be that this small detail reveals his father's lack of confidence in him?[64]

Think about the impact of hearing words like "You can't do anything right!" or "You're stupid!" from a parent. Such messages create wounds that fragment the soul. The irony was profound: Saul couldn't be trusted to lead donkeys, yet suddenly he was expected to lead an entire nation.

The truth is simple yet profound: You cannot lead your way out of shame!

This potentially explains Saul's behavior at his coronation. When called to be king, where was he? Saul had "hidden himself among the supplies" (1 Samuel 10:22). This wasn't humility; it was raw insecurity born from shame.

I've witnessed this pattern repeatedly with fallen leaders. I remember one prominent leader who used unhealthy coping mechanisms to mask his unresolved pain. When unpacked, he, too, carried deep childhood shame. Eventually, everything imploded and led to his ultimate removal from the organization. This could happen to any leader who carries unhealed wounds.

When you don't address the deep pain in your soul, you find ways to numb it, inevitably leading to poor decisions. The truth is simple yet profound: You cannot lead your way out of shame!

For Saul, the shame from his tribal background, family lineage, and his father's seeming lack of confidence in him deeply impacted his soul. Shame from these three sources was a sign of Saul's psychological trauma.

At the heart of Saul's struggles was what we might call the shame-fear-control cycle. This pattern begins when someone feels deeply ashamed about who they are at their core.[65] For Saul, this shame came from multiple sources. This shame then triggered fear that others would discover his perceived inadequacies and reject him.[66]

To handle this fear, Saul turned to control, attempting to manage his environment, circumstances, and the people around him to prevent his shame from being exposed. When his ability to control was threatened, he would either rebel against authority or withdraw to protect himself from further shame. For example, in 1 Samuel 13, Saul became fearful while waiting for Samuel to come and perform a sacrifice as he saw the people scattering from him. Saul rebelled against the command of the Lord and took it upon himself to offer the sacrifices. By the Lord's instructions, this was a duty only a priest such as Samuel could perform. This act signaled the beginning of his demise.

This destructive cycle trapped Saul in a pattern that ultimately undermined his leadership, damaging his relationship with God and others. As referenced earlier, these unprocessed childhood wounds created a fractured soul as he entered into his kingship.

Consider Jeffrey Skilling, the former CEO of Enron. Under Skilling, Enron soared, becoming one of America's most admired corporations. But beneath the glossy success was a deeply insecure leader desperate to control perceptions of himself and his company. Skilling's relentless pursuit to hide vulnerabilities drove him into deception, fraud, and ultimately, disgrace.[67] Based on his actions, one can only surmise that like King Saul, Skilling built his leadership on a foundation of shame, fear, and control. His story prompts us to ask: What unaddressed wounds pushed a leader like Skilling to sacrifice integrity for illusion?

There's No Pain Like Rejection

Rejection is a fundamentally distressing experience.[68] People like Saul who are hypersensitive to rejection will do almost anything to avoid it. Social rejection activates the same parts of the brain as physical pain, and the two experiences look remarkably similar on brain scans.[69] In fact, rejection can become so severe it has a clinical name: rejection sensitive dysphoria (RSD). According to the Cleveland Clinic, this is when "someone experiences severe emotional pain because of a failure or feeling rejected."[70]

I had a friend with whom I tried to connect on a deeper level. Yet, just as we seemed to be getting candid in a helpful way, he'd pull back. It turns out, because of some childhood wounds, he felt the need to reject people before they could reject him. Trauma, rather than wholeness, controlled his relationships.

Similarly, this same fear explains why King Saul, despite being anointed by God and possessing many leadership gifts, was intensely afraid of being rejected by others. Saul's fear of people's rejection ultimately proved much stronger than his fear of God's displeasure. As Saul admitted to Samuel, "I have sinned. I violated the LORD's command and your instructions. I was afraid of the men and so I gave in to them" (1 Samuel

15:24). How many times are we tempted to violate our leadership convictions and principles to please people? Like Saul, this gets us into trouble.

We can clearly see the unhealthy shame-fear-control cycle playing out in Saul's life. His shame about factors largely beyond his control caused him to reject himself. He then expected others to reject him too. This anticipation of rejection filled him with a fear of people. Saul strived to manage this fear by constantly trying to please others. The unfortunate result of Saul's fear of rejection was that he eventually was rejected by the man he admired most, Samuel (1 Samuel 15:35).

Samuel was a father figure to Saul. Time and again, Saul sought his blessing before making decisions or entering conflicts. Yet, because of his fear of people, Saul chose to please the crowd and avoid rejection rather than heed Samuel's wisdom or obey God's direction. This failure to lead properly led to an even greater rejection: the loss of God's approval to rule over Israel (1 Samuel 15:26). Rejection is what sent Saul into his downward spiral, leading to his final ruin. His army was defeated by the Philistines, and fearing capture, Saul took his own life (1 Samuel 31:1–6). Saul's breakdown and ultimate demise show his rejection sensitivity had reached a traumatic level with the worst possible outcome. How often do leaders face problems because they won't deal with their fear of rejection?

Looking at King Saul's story, we can see that even someone chosen by God and given special gifts can go through deeply wounding experiences. This suggests that no matter how blessed or talented we are, we're still human and vulnerable to trauma. Trauma that goes unnoticed and continues without understanding from others is called "disenfranchised trauma."

This includes emotional wounds like rejection and when others dismiss or minimize the pain someone is experiencing.[71] The good news is that with God's healing and by properly working through our painful experiences, we can find restoration and wholeness again.

Poor Decisions, Devastating Outcomes

Leader to leader, how are you doing? Has there been a time in your life and leadership when you felt unnoticed or misunderstood? Or is there trauma in your past that may be driving more of your present decisions than you realize?

Like Saul, leaders today with unprocessed trauma risk making harmful decisions from their wounded places. Remember, our study found a staggering 93.7 percent of American leaders have experienced trauma![72] This raises the stakes because instead of properly guiding their teams, wounded leaders may look to people or accomplishments to fill the emotional voids caused by trauma. This unhealthy dynamic eventually leads to damaged leaders, divided teams, and diminished vision.

The Billionaire Who Unraveled

At just nineteen, Elizabeth Holmes dropped out of Stanford to found her now-infamous company, Theranos. She convinced the world that her technology could "perform over 200 blood tests from a single drop of blood."[73] Hailed as Silicon Valley's next Steve Jobs, she raised $724 million from investors, with Theranos eventually reaching a $10 billion valuation.[74] By the time she was thirty, *Forbes* had named Holmes the youngest self-made female billionaire in United States history.[75]

The problem? She was lying. And in 2015, her legend began to unravel. Investigative journalists and regulatory scrutiny revealed that Theranos's claims were false. The company's blood-testing technology was unviable, and Holmes had misled investors, regulators, and partners about its capabilities. Internal whistleblowers and media reports exposed the deception, leading to criminal charges of fraud.[76]

She was sentenced to eleven years in prison. As of today, she's still incarcerated with a net worth of $0. Her rise was quick, but her downfall was even quicker. In hindsight, it's clear she had gotten herself in over her head. One falsehood led to another until she was too deep in the quicksand of lies to escape.

Yet, beneath the surface, more insidious factors lurked: Holmes was a traumatized leader. A psychiatrist who'd known Holmes since childhood described her as "an emotionally withdrawn child of a once-illustrious family being driven by a jealous mother who wanted her daughter to make a name for herself."[77] She was a child whose mother demanded she become an adult at a young age. Her mother's approval only came after exceptional performances.

Worse, she experienced diabolical abuse in college. Holmes testified under oath: "I was [assaulted] when I was at Stanford, and I decided to put myself into building Theranos. I wasn't going to class, and I was questioning how I was going to process that experience. And I decided that I was going to build a life by building this company."[78] Her entire life became a reaction to trauma.

Holmes also testified that her former romantic partner and Theranos COO, Ramesh "Sunny" Balwani, was abusive and exerted controlling influence over her personal and professional life.[79] She described how Balwani berated her, dictated her actions, and told her she needed to "kill the person that I was to become what he called 'the new Elizabeth.'"[80] Balwani has denied these allegations, but Holmes' testimony painted a picture of ongoing trauma and manipulation during her years running Theranos.

Her story is another tragedy of a promising, talented leader affected by traumatic fragmentation. Whether she realized it or not, trauma became a dominating force in her life and leadership. In the end, her leadership influence left a wake of destruction, hurting herself, those she led, and the investors who entrusted her with hundreds of millions of dollars.

Thank God her story isn't over. Holmes still has time to process her trauma and find healing for her soul. Her life continues to hold potential for great things. No matter where you are, a path to wholeness through soul leadership exists for you.

Breaking the Cycle of Traumatized Leadership

King Saul's story serves as a powerful warning about the devastating consequences of unprocessed trauma in leadership. From his tribal shame and family wounds to his fear-driven decisions and eventual suicide, we witness the complete unraveling of a leader who had considerable advantages at the start. Like the more recent examples of Bron Clifford, Jeffrey Skilling, and Elizabeth Holmes, Saul showed us that talent, promise, and position cannot overcome the destructive force of unprocessed psychological trauma.

The shame-fear-control cycle trapped Saul in a pattern that destroyed not only his own life but damaged his family, fractured his government, and nearly annihilated his nation. His rejection sensitivity led to increasingly desperate attempts to maintain control, culminating in madness, isolation, and self-deception. What began as childhood wounds festered into leadership failures with national consequences.

Yet Saul's tragic end was not inevitable. At multiple points throughout his story, opportunities for healing and redemption presented themselves. Had he chosen humility over pride, truth over deception, and connection over isolation, his story might have unfolded very differently.

As leaders, we all carry wounds. Leadership itself often exposes and exacerbates our deepest vulnerabilities. The pressures of responsibility, visibility, and decision-making can activate our traumatic responses in ways that impact everyone around us. The question is not whether we will face pain in leadership, but how we will respond to that pain.

The pressures of responsibility, visibility, and decision-making can activate our traumatic responses in ways that impact everyone around us.

In the next chapter, we'll explore why leadership pain is inevitable and how to handle it constructively. We'll discover practical pathways toward healing and wholeness that Saul never took—approaches that transform wounds into wisdom and brokenness into breakthrough. Unlike Saul, we can choose to face our trauma directly, process our pain honestly, and emerge as more authentic and effective leaders. We'll examine how soul leadership offers a way to break the destructive cycles that entrapped Saul and establish healthier patterns that lead to flourishing for ourselves and those we serve.

The tragedy of Saul reminds us what's at stake. Unlike Saul's story, ours is still being written. With the right understanding and tools, we can write a different ending—one of healing, redemption, and lasting influence.

CHAPTER 4

Navigating Pain

It was February 2010. I was halfway through preaching the fourth service of the weekend when it happened. Standing before our congregation, words that had always flowed suddenly died in my throat. While leading a fast-growing church at forty-one years old, something cracked.

The sanctuary lights seemed too bright. The faces before me blurred. My hands trembled against the pulpit as a wave of overwhelming emotion crashed over me, threatening to pull me under.

This isn't like me, I thought, as panic set in. *I think I'm losing it.*

Yet my body betrayed what my mind refused to accept. For nearly five years, I'd carried a weight that had finally cracked my soul. It started in the aftermath of Hurricane Katrina in 2005, and continued as I led through several years of relief and rebuilding efforts. Then, in the spring of 2008, we launched an ambitious three-year capital campaign to build a 2,700-seat auditorium on 65 acres. It started in spectacular fashion. The excitement of planning our new church building, coupled with the momentum of $20 million in pledges on a $40 million project, was electric. Then came the financial crash of fall 2008—the worst monetary crisis in seventy-five years.

Our elders and I gathered to discuss the devastating news: Our loan had been pulled, and we now needed to raise $25 million before any bank would consider financing the backend of the project. I suffered restless nights for months, lying awake, recalculating how we could possibly raise that much money in the middle of a global recession. The numbers simply wouldn't add up. Sunday mornings were especially difficult as I looked out at our congregation. I knew that behind those faithful faces were people experiencing foreclosures, bankruptcies, and shattered dreams.

Two questions haunted me, growing louder each day until they became a deafening roar I could no longer ignore: Did we miss God in this building campaign? How could I possibly ask people to honor pledges while they were losing their businesses and livelihoods?

Standing there that Sunday in February 2010, those questions finally consumed me. My vision blurred. My next words vanished. With shaking legs, I stepped away from the stage, walked straight to our executive pastor and whispered words I never thought I'd say: "I can't do this anymore."

What followed was a haze. My wife Jennifer's firm hand was in mine as she led me to the car after service. I remember the quiet determination in her voice as she called a babysitter. We immediately departed for a three-day trip so I could regain my bearings and discuss what next steps should be taken. During the two-and-a-half-hour drive to Fairhope, Alabama, I was barely able to speak. My sobbing was uncontrollable and lasted for forty-eight hours. There I was, a man known for emotional fortitude, boundless energy, and decisive leadership, curled up and confused.

"I'm done," I told Jennifer between ragged breaths. "I can't do this anymore. I've hit the wall." While there were no moral indiscretions or ethical compromises, I'd simply come to the end of my ability to cope with the chronic stress, demanding pressures, and cumulative trauma of driving hard for five years from one crisis to another.

Thank God my wife, our church elders, and overseers helped me take the first painful steps toward healing. They created a supportive circle around me, adjusting my responsibilities and finding a therapist who understood the unique pressures of leadership. What I couldn't see in those dark days was that my burnout would become a long, challenging, but ultimately redemptive eighteen-month journey back to wholeness. Often, God's greatest work begins precisely at the moment we think all is lost.

Often, God's greatest work begins precisely at the moment we think all is lost.

What I couldn't see then was that this painful journey was leading me toward *shalom*. The goal of soul leadership is *shalom*—a complete wholeness that stands in direct opposition to the fragmentation trauma creates. My journey back wasn't just about recovery; it was about restoration to the integrated leadership God intended.

This painful season taught me that when a crisis strikes, a leader's recovery or collapse often depends on two factors: the support system they've built and the healthy habits they've established beforehand. Thank God, by His grace, both were in place for me.

I shudder to think where my life and family would be without them. I was a hairsbreadth from leaving my calling and exiting the ministry entirely. This taught me how essential it is for leaders to recognize and address their pain and trauma before it completely fractures their ability to lead effectively.

Looking back now, I can see the warning signs that preceded my collapse, signals I ignored or rationalized away. Had I recognized these earlier, perhaps I could have sought help before reaching a breaking point. My experience isn't unique. Leaders show warning signs of burnout and trauma long before they hit their breaking point. Spotting these early signals is key to leadership that lasts.

Warning Signs

By now, we know that psychological trauma is a serious problem. But it's *unprocessed* trauma that is the greatest threat to a leader's emotional and psychological health. So, you may be wondering: *How do I know if I'm experiencing unprocessed trauma?* This is a key question for every person, especially leaders. As our *Leaders and Trauma Today* study found, 40 percent of American leaders experienced their most recent traumatic experience, adversity, or prolonged period of high stress within the last year alone![81]

To help answer this question, imagine your life is like a road trip. You're driving through a beautiful countryside, dealing with children who want to know if you're there yet, and trying to make good time! Yet, if you don't pay attention to your dashboard, you can miss a critical piece of information that affects your entire trip: the check engine light.

When your check engine light pops on, you know there's a problem. Yet you often do not know what it is. At this point in your journey, it's time to pull over and look at the dashboard of your life. Unprocessed trauma is typically unconscious and below the surface. This means it's hard to know what's really going on with your psychological and physical health as they relate to trauma. Yet, just like a check engine light, there are signs to watch out for. As you read this list, note any that pertain to you.[82]

Emotional and Psychological Warning Signs

- **Persistent Anxiety and Hypervigilance:** Feeling constantly on edge, overly alert to potential threats even in safe environments, leading to exhaustion and overwhelm.
- **Intrusive Thoughts, Flashbacks, and Memories:** Re-experiencing traumatic events vividly, as if they are happening in the present, causing intense distress and trouble focusing.
- **Difficulty Regulating Emotions:** Experiencing sudden angry outbursts, irritability, or emotional instability without clear triggers.
- **Sense of Impending Doom:** Persistent feeling that something terrible is about to happen, even in objectively safe situations.
- **Avoidance Behavior:** Steering clear of places, people, or activities that remind you of the trauma, which can limit your quality of life.

- **Emotional Numbing or Detachment:** Feeling disconnected from your emotions or surroundings, which can hinder your ability to experience joy or intimacy.
- **Dissociation:** Experiencing a sense of numbness, detachment, or feeling disconnected from reality.
- **Low Self-Esteem, Shame, Guilt, and Self-Blame:** Persistent negative beliefs about yourself related to the trauma.
- **Depression and Feelings of Hopelessness:** Ongoing sadness, hopelessness, or withdrawal from activities once enjoyed.
- **Trust Issues and Intimacy Challenges:** Difficulty trusting others or forming close relationships, often stemming from past abuse or neglect.
- **Codependency and People-Pleasing:** Overly dependent on others or excessively trying to please to avoid conflict or abandonment.
- **Self-Destructive Behaviors:** Engaging in substance abuse, self-harm, or reckless behaviors as unhealthy coping mechanisms.

Physical Warning Signs

- **Sleep Disturbances:** Difficulty falling or staying asleep, nightmares related to trauma.
- **Somatic Symptoms:** Sensations such as physical pain, physical discomfort, and insomnia that trigger physical reaction patterns developed because of trauma.
- **Chronic Physical Issues:** Headaches, stomachaches, muscle tension, heart palpitations, sweating, shaking, or other unexplained physical pain.

Behavioral Warning Signs

- **Lack of Motivation or Feeling "Stuck":** Difficulty initiating tasks or moving forward in life, often linked to feelings of helplessness or abandonment.
- **Hypersensitivity to Others:** Feeling easily attacked or triggered by benign comments or actions from others.
- **Social Withdrawal and Isolation:** Avoiding social interactions or isolating oneself from friends and family.
- **Overcontrol:** Setting rigid boundaries, being overly self-protective, struggling with ambiguity, and being unwilling to take risks.[83]

To be clear, just because you are experiencing one or more of these warning signs does not automatically mean you have unprocessed trauma. These can all point to other problems such as extreme exhaustion. However, they can be warning signs of unprocessed trauma and it would be wise to consult a mental health professional if yzou are repeatedly experiencing a number of those symptoms listed above.

As we've established: Traumatized leaders are at a much higher risk of negatively affecting those they influence. Forty-five percent of leaders in America say they have unintentionally hurt someone they were leading because of their unhealed traumatic experiences, adversity, or prolonged periods of high stress.[84] Recognizing trauma is your first major step toward wholeness. The rest of this book will help you discover what to do about it. It's crucial to know if you have unprocessed trauma. It's also critical to understand what the pathway for recovery looks like.

Revisiting the Stress Continuum

After my burnout in 2010, I reluctantly visited a psychotherapist in another state. I'd never done anything like this before and was unsure of what to expect. I showed up with the brim of my hat pulled down and wearing dark sunglasses. I know that sounds strange, but boy I felt vulnerable. I just wanted my anonymity. After all, who wants to know their pastor is visiting a psychotherapist? At least, that was my thinking at the time. Today, I'm happy to talk about my seasons of counseling, hopefully encouraging any leader to get help amidst a crisis.

I stopped abruptly at the office door before walking in. I just couldn't get over the "psycho" in "psychotherapist." I'd never even heard of a psychotherapist before. It reminded me of the Alfred Hitchcock thriller *Psycho*. I wondered why he couldn't have called himself a life coach. Yet my recovery began inside of that office.

In addition to therapy, one of the most helpful books I read on my healing journey was Wayne Cordeiro's *Leading on Empty*.[85] It helped me see the progression I'd been on for five years up to that point. I learned that the operative word in my condition at the time was *stress*.

Remember the stress continuum from chapter 1? You can think of it like a traffic light. Green is the healthy stress zone, which tells you to go. Yellow is the chronic stress zone, which advises: "Proceed with caution; you're entering risky territory, and you can't live there." And red means stop, because you're going to crash! The stress continuum holds a key to understanding where I was and where you might be right now. Are you in a healthy place where growth can take place? Or are you at the crossroads of compounding stress?

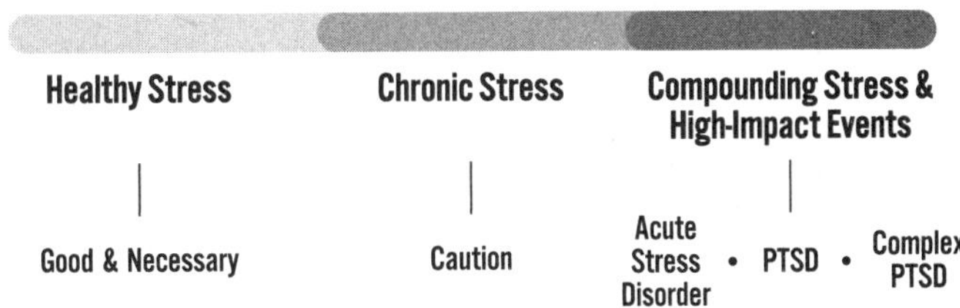

Healthy Stress Zone (Green Light)

The healthy stress zone refers to the positive, motivating stress that helps us grow, learn, and adapt. Just like muscles that get stronger after a good workout, healthy stress challenges us enough to stimulate growth, but not so much that it overwhelms us. It's the kind of stress that pushes us out of our comfort zones, increases our capacity to handle adversity, boosts creativity, and aids in personal development.[86]

Healthy stress, called eustress, acts as a catalyst that energizes us, sharpens our focus, and prepares us to meet challenges head-on. It's temporary, manageable, and balanced by our ability to recover and bounce back. In this zone, stress feels like a helpful companion rather than a debilitating burden.

Here are some signals you're in the healthy zone:[87]

- **You Are Energized and Focused:** Instead of feeling drained or overwhelmed, you notice a boost in energy and mental clarity. Your mind is alert, and you're able to concentrate on tasks effectively.

- **Challenges Feel Manageable:** The obstacles or demands you face feel challenging yet achievable. You recognize that while things require effort, you have the resources and skills to handle them.
- **Motivation and Drive Increase:** You feel inspired to take action, try new things, or push yourself a bit further. There's a sense of excitement or curiosity about what you can accomplish.
- **You Experience Positive Physical Responses:** Your body may show signs of activation—like a faster heartbeat or slight adrenaline rush—but these sensations feel invigorating rather than frightening or exhausting.
- **You Bounce Back Quickly:** After completing a stressful task or event, you recover well. You can relax, recharge, and return to baseline without lingering fatigue or emotional distress.
- **You Notice Growth and Learning:** You recognize stress is helping you develop new skills, insights, or confidence. You feel a sense of accomplishment and progress.
- **You Maintain Emotional Balance:** While you might feel pressure or discomfort, it doesn't overwhelm you or tip into anxiety and irritability. Your emotions remain within a healthy range.
- **You Build Healthy Relationships:** Stress doesn't cause you to withdraw or lash out. You're able to communicate effectively, build healthy connections, and seek support when needed.

- **You Sleep Well and Practice Self-Care:** Despite the challenges, your sleep patterns and self-care routines stay intact, supporting your overall well-being.

Healthy stress is essential for growth. Stanford psychologist Kelly McGonigal explained it this way: "One simple mindset reset that can help us face and find the good in the stress in our lives is to view it as an opportunity to learn and grow. The ability to learn from stress is built into the basic biology of the stress response. For several hours after you have a strong stress response, the brain is rewiring itself to remember and learn from the experience. Stress leaves an imprint on your brain that prepares you to handle similar stress the next time you encounter it."[88]

Healthy stress encourages us to stretch our limits, adapt to new situations, and build resilience. Without it, life can become stagnant and unmotivating. The key is to stay within this healthy zone as much as possible. Here, stress is a tool for growth rather than a source of harm. For me, setting a full and balanced daily agenda brings with it an appropriate level of stress and challenge. At the end of the day, I feel a deep sense of satisfaction, which motivates me to wake up ready to tackle the new day.

Those who are operating in the healthy stress zone have the capacity and ability to absorb crises without tilting. At times, life events will move us out of this zone. Emergencies happen, and our plate can become overfull. Yet, by recognizing these signals, you can regulate stress in your life and avoid slipping into the chronic or traumatic stress zones, where stress becomes overwhelming or damaging.

Chronic Stress Zone (Yellow Light)

Several years ago I visited Israel. The experience was profound. I walked where Jesus walked, following the ancient road to Emmaus as it stretched through the Judaean mountains. Further north, stones worn smooth by centuries of travelers supported our steps as we scaled the strategic heights of Golan and trekked the slopes of Mount Hermon. It was sacred ground beneath my feet.

My shoes, however, were wrong for the journey. With each step on the unforgiving terrain, damage accumulated in my right foot. Yet I ignored it and pushed through the pain for two weeks until a stress fracture formed. Still, I pressed on, unwilling to acknowledge what my body was trying to tell me: "Steve, stop to get some new shoes!"

Over the next few weeks, the damage spread as my left knee began to ache, overcompensating for my injured right foot. In the same way, one unaddressed area of chronic stress created another in a physical analogy—wounds left untreated seldom stay contained. Instead, they spread through interconnected systems. What began as discomfort in my foot now hobbled me almost entirely, all because I refused to stop to take care of a single issue.

That's the insidious nature of a seemingly small injury. It doesn't break you completely. You can still function and make it through the day. Yet you're compromised. Performance suffers. If you don't address the underlying problem, healing never happens. The problem just worsens, spreading its web of pain wider with each step.

Our brains experience similar injuries under chronic stress. The chronic stress zone is the cautionary stage where stress shifts from being manageable to becoming a persistent burden that gradually wears down your physical and mental health. Unlike healthy stress, chronic stress lingers, slowly draining your psychological resources and causing damage to your brain and body over time. This stage is often the breeding ground for anxiety, burnout, depression, and other health problems.

Chronic stress feels like being stuck in a pressure cooker where you experience constant tension without adequate relief or recovery. It may arise from ongoing challenges such as work overload, financial strain, difficult relationships, unresolved personal issues, and more.

Here are some warning signs you're in the chronic zone:[89]

- **Physical Symptoms:** Frequent headaches, muscle tension (especially in your neck, shoulders, and back), gastrointestinal issues (nausea, diarrhea, constipation), chest tightness, rapid heartbeat, fatigue, changes in appetite or weight, and disrupted sleep patterns such as insomnia or excessive sleepiness
- **Cognitive Symptoms:** Difficulty concentrating, forgetfulness, mental fog or clouded thinking, indecision, negative thinking patterns, and reduced problem-solving ability
- **Emotional Symptoms:** Irritability, anxiety, feeling helpless or overwhelmed, withdrawal, mood swings, low motivation, and increased feelings of sadness or frustration
- **Behavioral Symptoms:** Social withdrawal or isolation, procrastination, neglecting responsibilities, excessive use of alcohol, tobacco, or drugs as coping mechanisms, changes in eating habits, and reduced physical activity

- **Burnout Indicators:** Feeling emotionally drained and physically exhausted despite rest, cynicism or detachment from work or relationships, lowered sense of accomplishment, and loss of motivation or hope[90]

Chronic stress is not just "in your head." When we live in chronic stress, our bodies keep pumping out cortisol and adrenaline—stress hormones we were never meant to carry at elevated levels long-term.[91] Over time, they overload us and keep our nervous system stuck in overdrive. This can lead to serious physical health consequences, including cardiovascular disease, immune dysfunction, obesity,[92] digestive disorders, and mental health conditions like anxiety and depression.[93] Recognizing these signs early allows you to take steps to reduce stress, seek support, and prevent progression to more severe states.

I experienced chronic stress in those post-Katrina years. With three young children, a growing church, managing a building campaign during an economic recession, and trying to finish graduate school, I could never fully relax. Though my body sent warning signals like constant headaches and stomach issues, I didn't listen. Now, I'm not suggesting people quit their current responsibilities—many of you are in necessary building phases of life. But there's a way to work smarter rather than harder, following that old wisdom: Measure twice, cut once.

I recognize there are different life seasons and periods of intense pressure. Seasons of press are inevitable, but they shouldn't become your permanent residence. The chronic stress zone is a caution sign, not a badge of honor. Pay attention to these warning signals as they're your body and brain's way of telling you that something needs to change before the fractures spread.

Sometimes circumstances beyond our control push us into dangerous areas of stress—as Hurricane Katrina did for me. Yet it's important to note that we can also end up in the chronic stress zone through the decisions we make. We have the responsibility to say "no" to opportunities, expectations, and demands that consistently pull our souls into unhealthy levels of chronic stress. Saying "no" gracefully is a vital skill that helps you stay in control of your schedule and remain in the healthy stress zone.

Traumatic Stress Zone (Red Light)

The traumatic stress zone represents the most severe level of stress where its intensity and duration overwhelm your ability to cope. This zone includes acute trauma reactions and long-term disorders that can profoundly disrupt brain function, emotional regulation, and daily life. Stress here is no longer adaptive; it becomes harmful and often requires professional intervention.

At my therapist's office, I was getting help for this exact issue. He became my unexpected guide through the fog of burnout. Inside that office, he explained to me how the chronic stressors and crises over the course of my life had finally reached a stage of trauma. I was like that proverbial frog in the kettle—slowly boiling without realizing it—until the road of pain and exhaustion led me straight to his door.

I'll never forget when he looked at me over his glasses and said, "Take off the cape, Superman. You can't do everything." Much of my identity in life was based on helping and leading others, and I had reached a breaking point. This was the traumatic stress zone of the stress continuum. And it was time to do something about it.

The Trauma Spectrum

Acute Stress Disorder • PTSD • Complex PTSD

Trauma disorders exist on a spectrum defined primarily by duration and intensity rather than distinct symptom sets. While acute stress disorder (ASD), post-traumatic stress disorder (PTSD), and complex PTSD (CPTSD) share core symptoms, they differ in their development and severity.

ASD represents the initial trauma response, occurring within the first month after exposure to a traumatic event such as natural disasters, assaults, accidents, or life-threatening situations.[94] If symptoms persist beyond one month, the diagnosis shifts to PTSD.

PTSD develops when trauma symptoms continue beyond one month and significantly impair functioning.[95] Without treatment, these symptoms can become chronic and debilitating.

CPTSD stems from prolonged or repeated traumatic events.[96] While sharing core PTSD symptoms, CPTSD includes additional challenges with emotional regulation, self-conception, and relationships.

Stress in the traumatic zone isn't just feeling overwhelmed; it actually changes your brain structure and affects your body. It's like an internal alarm system that stays permanently switched on, making you jumpy one moment and numb the next. Everyday tasks like making decisions or maintaining relationships become huge challenges. Your body can show the strain, too, with problems like chronic pain, poor sleep, and weakened immunity. This isn't just having a bad day. Your whole system is in crisis. Without proper help, these trauma disorders can take over your life, which is why reaching out to a professional may not be optional but essential for finding your way back to health.

Leadership Pain

So, what zone are you in? You could be thriving in the healthy stress zone, experiencing vitality and focus. Some of you may think you're okay but have been pressing past danger points in the chronic stress zone, leaving yourself vulnerable to worsening conditions. Or, you might be limping and wounded in the traumatic stress zone, desperately searching for a way forward.

I assure you, there is hope. There's a pathway back to health and wholeness; you don't have to end up where I did. You can start mitigating the effects of stress-induced trauma right now.

Unaddressed trauma doesn't simply disappear. Instead, it manifests in our leadership patterns and affects how we make decisions and build relationships. Understanding how early life experiences shape these patterns is crucial for breaking free from destructive cycles.

Moving Forward

Understanding where you fall on the stress continuum—whether in the healthy, chronic, or traumatic zones—is crucial for your leadership journey. While stress disorders such as ASD, PTSD, and CPTSD can feel overwhelming, there is genuine hope for healing and growth.

That Sunday in 2010, when I broke down at the pulpit, wasn't the end of my story—it was the beginning of something new. Even with healing possible, buried trauma can still plant hidden land mines along your leadership path. In the next chapter, we'll explore how these emotional land mines operate in our lives, creating what I call the "Trauma-Triggers Effect." We'll discover how unprocessed trauma can hijack our leadership at the worst possible moments, and most importantly, how to recognize the caution signs before they undermine our effectiveness and damage those we lead.

CHAPTER 5

Traumas, Triggers, and Terrible Habits

I can see the desert sun beat down with relentless intensity. Moses wiped sweat from his brow, the weight of leadership pressing on him like the heat. Though he'd led his people through countless trials, the past weeks had worn him particularly thin. His sister Miriam's death left a void that ached constantly (Numbers 20:1). It was one more loss in a life defined by loss from its very beginning. As a baby, his mother was forced to give him up to save him from the genocide of Hebrew children in Egypt.

"Moses!" The shout from outside his tent carried the now-familiar tone of complaint. Because "there was no water for the congregation; so they gathered together against Moses and Aaron" (Numbers 20:2 NKJV).

They continued, "Why have you brought up the assembly of the LORD into this wilderness, that we and our animals should die here? And why have you made us come up out of Egypt, to bring us to this evil place? It is not a place of grain or figs or vines or pomegranates; nor is there any water to drink" (Numbers 20:4–5 NKJV).

His head throbbed as he stepped into the blinding sunlight. The crowd that had gathered looked angry and desperate. This wasn't the first time they'd faced water shortages, but the timing couldn't have been worse. Grief had hollowed him out, leaving raw edges where his patience should have been resolute.

As the people brought their complaints and accusations, Moses felt something snap inside him, a trigger point pressed once too often. This wasn't the first time Moses's anger had been activated with costly consequences. His leadership journey was marked by explosive reactions in moments of pressure. Years earlier, seeing an Egyptian beating a Hebrew slave, Moses had been so consumed by rage that he killed the Egyptian and hid his body in the sand (Exodus 2:11–12). That triggered reaction cost him forty years in the wilderness of Midian. The irony wasn't lost on Moses that he had been raised in the palace of the very man—Pharaoh—who had ordered the genocide of Hebrew baby boys. Being raised under the roof of the man responsible for killing his people had planted deep-seated trauma within him that would periodically resurface throughout his leadership journey.

The grief of Miriam's death, the legitimate need for water, and now these personal attacks converged like a perfect storm in his soul. He exchanged a glance with his brother Aaron before retreating to the tabernacle. There, they fell on their faces before the Lord, seeking direction. God's response was clear: "Take the rod; you and your brother Aaron gather the congregation together. Speak to the rock before their eyes, and it will yield its water; thus you shall bring water for them out of the rock, and give drink to the congregation and their animals" (Numbers 20:8 NKJV).

Simple instructions: grab the staff, gather the people, and *speak* to the rock. Yet as Moses stood before the assembled Israelites, something else was churning within him. The faces before him blurred with his pain, their complaints echoing in his mind not as a legitimate need but as a personal attack. Decades of his faithfulness reduced to this moment of contempt by the people.

The trigger was pulled . . .

"Hear now, you rebels! Must we bring water for you out of this rock?" he asked sharply (Numbers 20:10 NKJV).

Then, instead of speaking to the rock as God had instructed, Moses lifted his arm and struck it—not once, but twice—the staff cracking against stone with all the force of his pent-up anger and frustration.

Water burst forth abundantly. The people drank. Their livestock drank. The immediate crisis was resolved. Yet the damage was done.

"But the LORD said to Moses and Aaron, 'Because you did not trust me enough to demonstrate my holiness to the people of Israel, you will not lead them into the land I am giving them!'" (Numbers 20:12 NLT).

In a single triggered moment, the leader who had guided a nation from slavery to freedom lost his own opportunity to enter the promised land. His momentary dysregulation and sin—a familiar trauma response that bypassed his rational judgment—altered the trajectory of his life. This is one of the hidden dangers of unprocessed trauma in leadership.

The more influence we have, the greater the consequences when our emotional brain hijacks our rational thinking, resulting in compromised leadership. In this passage, we see how Moses's poor leadership resulted in collateral damage, costing his brother, Aaron, the opportunity to enter the promised land!

The more influence we have, the greater the consequences when our emotional brain hijacks our rational thinking, resulting in compromised leadership.

Moses's pattern of triggered responses appeared repeatedly throughout his leadership. When he descended Mount Sinai to find the people worshiping a golden calf, his anger burned hot. He threw down the Ten Commandments God wrote on stone tablets, shattering them at the foot of the mountain (Exodus 32:19).

Even after years of walking closely with God, Moses still struggled with the anger issues bubbling under the surface of his leadership. What you don't work out, you act out. Ultimately, his failure to deal with his underlying trauma cost him his leadership destiny. He would guide the people to the edge of the promised land but fail to enter himself. His momentary triggered response of striking the rock revealed what remained unhealed in his soul.

Moses isn't alone. His story reveals a pattern that plays out in boardrooms, classrooms, and living rooms every day. I think back to the times in my life when I said regrettable things in a moment of anger to my wife, children, teammates, and friends. As I've heard it said, for every rip, there needs to be a repair.

While forgiveness is granted by most, trust must be rebuilt over time.

When people carry unhealed wounds, those wounds eventually speak—often with devastating consequences. This is why soul leadership begins with stewarding your inner landscape, tending to your state of wholeness or fragmentation.

The first component of the soul leadership cycle is awareness of the trauma-triggers effect. This unhealthy pattern occurs when people carry unprocessed trauma, creating hidden land mines that explode unexpectedly in high-pressure situations. These land mines are called triggers, or being "activated," which are catalysts leading to heightened states of emotional reactivity.

When Trauma Fires Without Warning

A trigger is like an emotional alarm that goes off in your brain when something reminds you of past hurt. When triggered, or activated, your emotional brain overpowers your thinking brain. This happens automatically, without you choosing it.[97] In fact, that lack of choice is part of the point! It works this way because at some point in the past, we were in such great danger or under such extreme stress that our body knew we didn't have time for (or couldn't create) measured, thoughtful responses.

When a flash flood is crashing toward us, we have to run. If a lion is stalking us, we don't have time for a list of pros and cons. Our limbic system detects the threat and instantly activates our nervous system. It's our automatic emergency response system, and it fires in milliseconds. Our body sounds the alarm and our nervous system helps us to flee to escape, freeze to avoid being seen, fight to defend ourselves, or fawn to diffuse a dangerous situation. Our nervous system can sense a threat so quickly that we often term it "instinct" or "listening to your gut" It's a miraculous, effective survival mechanism.

Trauma may explain triggered behavior, but it doesn't excuse it.

If the event was traumatic enough, our nervous system is conditioned by it and remembers what happened. It will now react to things that look or feel similar. If we've been bitten by a snake, we are more likely to startle when our peripheral vision sees an extension cord in the grass. If your home was ever broken into during the night, dark rooms are much more likely to put you on edge. That's your body being conditioned by a past traumatic event and signaling you that the situation now seems similar to the one where you were hurt. It's a trigger.[98]

Trauma may explain triggered behavior, but it doesn't excuse it. We must take ownership of our actions in order to heal and recover from trauma.

Our Actions, Our Responsibility

For leaders, this is especially dangerous because triggered reactions can damage relationships, lead to poor decisions, and undermine your influence. These reactions are signs that old trauma needs healing. They're like warning lights on your leadership dashboard that shouldn't be ignored. Here are the stakes: *Not dealing with your triggers costs your leadership influence.*

When someone is carrying deep wounds, it often takes remarkably little to trigger them and transport them back to their original pain, bypassing rational thought entirely. In these moments, the emotional brain (limbic system) hijacks the logical brain (prefrontal cortex), and what follows isn't a measured response but rather a survival reaction from past pain that refuses to stay buried.

Being easily triggered, or activated, is one of the greatest indications of unprocessed trauma in the life of an individual.[99] Physiologically, a trigger can be a negative stimulus that shapes our thoughts and influences our responses. It sets off a memory tape or flashback, transporting you back to the event of your original trauma or hurtful experience.[100] As van der Kolk noted in *The Body Keeps the Score*, "the bottom line is that the threat-perception system of the brain has changed, and people's physical reactions are dictated by the imprint of the past."[101]

Not dealing with your triggers costs your leadership influence.

When your emotional brain hijacks your logical brain, this neurobiological takeover causes you to react from an emotionally dysregulated state rather than responding thoughtfully. Think of it like stepping on a landmine you didn't know was there. You're walking through life, handling your responsibilities and leading your team, when suddenly something happens that detonates an explosive emotional reaction within you. This reaction feels disproportionate even to you, yet it seems uncontrollable in the moment. As I've heard it said before, "When it's hysterical, it's historical."

It's like this: Your brain constantly processes information from your five primary senses. Under normal circumstances, this information flows smoothly between different brain regions.

However, when you encounter something that reminds your limbic system of past trauma, even subconsciously, the system breaks down. The very mental capabilities you need most as a leader—strategic thinking, emotional regulation, and interpersonal awareness—become compromised precisely when they're in highest demand.

Here's a simple illustration. Imagine you're driving down a familiar road. You approach an intersection where, five years ago, you witnessed a terrible accident. Though you haven't consciously thought about that accident in years, as you near the intersection, your heart rate increases, your palms begin to sweat, and you grip the steering wheel tighter. You may even slow down dramatically or change your route, all without consciously deciding to do so. That's a trigger in action—you're being activated.

For leaders, these triggers can be particularly problematic. The principal who explodes at a teacher for questioning their vision may be reacting not to the question itself but to emotional memories of being belittled in childhood. The pastor who micromanages every detail of church events may be responding to early trauma in which lack of control led to painful outcomes. The executive who struggles to delegate may be unconsciously triggered by early experiences where trust led to betrayal.

Triggers Are Personal

What's particularly challenging about triggers is their highly personalized nature. Remember, trauma is stored in the limbic system, not in the event itself. In other words, you carry the trauma far beyond the event. Psychological trauma is the result of a traumatic event combined with how a person uniquely experiences it.

This explains why different leaders can go through the same challenging situation yet respond in entirely different ways. This is a pattern I've seen time and again. One leader becomes defensive when their decisions are questioned because it triggers memories of a critical father. Another leader welcomes the same questioning as an opportunity for growth and improvement because their childhood experiences reinforced curiosity. Same stimulus, entirely different responses. One might remain calm and centered, while another becomes defensive or shuts down. The difference often lies in their personal trauma history and whether those experiences have been properly processed.

Moses's story illustrates this perfectly. The complaints about water weren't new. The Israelites had grumbled before (Exodus 17:3). What was different at Meribah was the confluence of factors that triggered Moses: his grief over Miriam's death, the pressure of the immediate crisis, and the accumulated weight of leading a difficult people.

Understanding the personalized nature of triggers gives us two critical insights. First, it helps us recognize that our trigger responses aren't always moral failings but neurobiological reactions to perceived threats. Second, it reminds us that healing must be equally personalized. We must take responsibility for our healing. There are multiple approaches to trauma recovery designed to meet individual therapeutic needs (discussed in chapter 9).

For every leader, identifying personal triggers is the first critical step toward effective soul leadership. Van der Kolk put it like this: "Sensing, naming, and identifying what is going on inside is the first step to recovery."[102] Without this awareness, we remain vulnerable to emotional takeovers that can diminish our effectiveness, damage our relationships, and derail our leadership.

Coping Mechanisms and Terrible Habits

The truth is, if we don't deal with our triggers, our triggers will deal with us. Unprocessed trauma often steers individuals toward destructive coping mechanisms like turning to excessive food or alcohol consumption, substance abuse, or even immoral sexual behaviors as ways to manage overwhelming emotions and numb the pain that triggers activate. These coping mechanisms are terrible habits and sinful responses. These unhealthy patterns don't just manifest in hidden addictive behaviors but also transform how we interact with others and navigate our daily lives.

When we allow unprocessed trauma to activate us repeatedly, we give territory in our lives to destructive patterns of behavior.

When we're triggered, we often respond like Moses did: We lash out, withdraw, become controlling, or engage in inordinate people-pleasing. These are attempts to manage the overwhelming emotions flooding our system. Over time, these emergency responses become habitual ways of functioning.

The apostle Paul recognized this danger when he wrote, "'Be angry, and do not sin': do not let the sun go down on your wrath, nor give place to the devil" (Ephesians 4:26–27 NKJV). The Greek word for "place" is *topos*, meaning territory.[103] When we allow unprocessed trauma to activate us repeatedly, we give territory in our lives to destructive patterns of behavior.

These unhealthy coping mechanisms develop gradually. What begins as an occasional emotional outburst can evolve into established behaviors that affect every area of life. As time passes without ownership of maladaptive behaviors, proper processing, and healing, these coping mechanisms become entrenched, often manifesting as:

- anxiety disorders[104]
- mood disorders[105]
- personality disorders[106]
- addictive behaviors[107]
- substance abuse
- pornography and sexual indiscretions
- emotional dysregulation[108]
- decision-making impairments[109]

For leaders, these coping mechanisms are particularly problematic. The leader whose unprocessed childhood rejection leads to approval addiction will often make decisions based on popularity rather than principle. The executive whose childhood trauma created hypervigilance might micromanage their team into disempowerment and indecision. The pastor whose early experiences of betrayal left him unable to trust may, under pressure, isolate himself from the very relationships he needs to thrive.

We call responses like these "pathologies," which you can regard as reactions that hurt more than they help. These survival mechanisms become unhealthy patterns of thinking, emotional response, and behaving. One helpful way to understand pathological responses is to recognize that at the time of their development they were coping mechanisms for survival. Yet, they often develop into self-destructive behaviors. The Bible teaches us that these harmful actions are called sin (Romans 6:12). And sin works its insidious tentacles into every aspect of our lives.

Think about King Saul. His unresolved trauma and insecurity created a pattern of terrible habits that eventually destroyed his reign. What began as occasional fear-based decisions spiraled into paranoia, jealousy, murderous rage, and eventual suicide. His triggered response to David's popularity, when the people sang, "Saul has slain his thousands, and David his tens of thousands" (1 Samuel 18:7), reveals how quickly our traumatized minds can catastrophize a situation.

Trauma ▸ Triggers ▸ Terrible Habits

Understanding this progression from trauma to triggers to terrible habits is essential for leaders. We must recognize that our disproportionate reactions to certain situations often stem from unprocessed wounds, not current circumstances.

This understanding doesn't excuse destructive behavior, but it does help explain it. And understanding and ownership are the first steps toward healing. When we recognize our personal triggers and understand how they're connected to past pain, we take the first crucial step toward transformation—*awareness*. By recognizing the connection between our past trauma, current triggers, and established habits, we can begin the deep soul work of healing and integration. This is soul leadership.

Breaking the Trauma-Triggers-Terrible Habits Loop

Moses's journey teaches us that even the greatest leaders can suffer from unprocessed trauma. His story serves as both a cautionary tale and a roadmap for our own leadership effectiveness. The path forward isn't simply trying harder or employing more willpower. It's gaining the tools and wisdom necessary to break the trauma-triggers-terrible habits loop. Healing trauma results in the integration of our fragmented selves and the restoration of healthy communication between our emotional and logical brain systems. But here's where many leaders fail: They attempt this journey alone.

The truth is that healing from trauma isn't a solo expedition. It requires safe relationships and support systems that hold us accountable while offering grace. Just as a financial reserve helps you weather unexpected expenses, emotional reserves built through healthy relationships prepare you for life's inevitable challenges.

Now that you've gained insight on what might be going on with you, in part two you'll find practical tools and strategies on where to go from here. This brings us to what we'll explore in the next chapter: the resilience equation.

PART 2

WHERE DO I GO FROM HERE?

CHAPTER 6

The Resilience Equation: Relationships

Imagine your life as a collection of bank accounts. Rather than just tracking dollars and cents, these accounts hold something far more valuable—your reserves. Each day, you're either making deposits or withdrawals, building up or depleting your reserves. These reserves create your ability to be resilient. Having enough money in the bank (reserves) allows you to bounce back in an emergency (resilience).

In the same way that we often have different bank accounts, we also have different life accounts: emotional, physical, spiritual, relational, and more. When these accounts are healthy and full, you're ready to face whatever challenges come your way.

Resilience isn't just about bouncing back from hard times. It is also about how well you can respond to challenges as they occur.[110] Our study found that 40 percent of leaders in America have experienced trauma, adversity, or prolonged periods of high stress within the last year.[111] There is an overwhelming need to build resilience! The goal of building resilience is ultimately about living and leading from wholeness.

Imagine your air conditioner breaks down in a heatwave, but you don't have the financial means to fix it. Because you didn't build reserves, you were only one breakdown away from real trouble. However, if you have financial margin, you can respond without crumbling.

In his groundbreaking book *Margin*, Richard Swenson introduced a simple yet profound concept: The difference between your load (what you carry) and your limits (your capacity) equals your margin.[112] When your expenses consistently exceed your income, you face financial crisis. Similarly, when your emotional and relational withdrawals consistently exceed your deposits, you face a resilience crisis. Having margin is a critical factor of resilience.

Resilience is both your capacity to handle adversity as it comes and then bounce back in a healthy way.[113] The trouble is, so many leaders live without any margin. This is why proactively building resilience is vital to enduring success.

The great news is that, just like financial reserves, anyone can build their mental and emotional resilience—regardless of personality traits. Building these reserves is mission-critical because the stress continuum we looked at earlier shows us what happens when we experience overwhelming levels of stress. Preparing ourselves beforehand can prevent crises from triggering things like acute stress disorder and post-traumatic stress disorder. A critical element of creating resilience, or your ability to rebound from crisis, is your relational support network.

As Super Bowl–winning NFL coach Tony Dungy wisely observed, "Personal relationships are the fertile soil from which all advancement, all success, all achievement in real life grows."[114]

These relationships represent some of your most significant deposits into your resilience accounts, which is why healthy relationships are the first part of the resilience equation.

You Can't Get Through This on Your Own

Years ago, my friend, Corey, experienced a parent's worst nightmare. His son came home describing a terrible car accident he'd witnessed. They later discovered the crash had claimed his other son's life. Grief tore through their family and community.

Without hesitation, his mentor flew across the country to be with them. Through tears, the mentor said to Corey, "You can't get through this on your own." The following months were incredibly difficult, but with support from his mentor, friends, family, and colleagues, they weathered this devastating storm. Without this [illegible] of support, my friend's organization would have be[illegible]erely impacted. Today, their organization thrives, and, most importantly, his family continues to heal.

Some burdens are simply too heavy to carry alone. More than personal wisdom, our need for connection is divinely designed. In Scripture, we find a profound statement about human nature: God said, "It is not good for the man to be alone" (Genesis 2:18). Now, this was before the fall, before sin entered the world. Adam was in perfect communion with God. Yet God looked at Adam, made in His image, and declared that continual solitude was "not good."

This tells us something crucial about our design: We were made for a relationship not just with God, but with one another. We are hardwired for connection and will not survive without it.[115]

Trauma and Our Need for Connection

Perhaps this is why isolation is one of the most devastating experiences we can face as humans. When we experience trauma—whether through loss, abuse, disaster, or other painful events—our need for genuine connection becomes even more critical. Research has consistently shown that social support is one of the strongest predictors of resilience after traumatic events. Remember, resilience is the ability to withstand and recover from difficulties.[116] Those who have meaningful relationships to turn to are more likely to recover and even experience post-traumatic growth.[117]

The reality is that trauma disrupts our sense of safety and belonging in the world. It can leave us feeling disconnected not only from others but from ourselves. In fact, our study found that 49 percent of leaders in the baby boomer generation say their past trauma has caused hyperindependence, in which they feel the need to handle everything themselves and rarely ask for help, even when they need it.[118] Since trauma has the tendency to produce isolation in our lives, the healing power of human connection becomes not just beneficial but essential.

The Impact of Relationships on Well-being

Loneliness has significant impacts on our health, including stress—both acute and chronic.[119] Being isolated isn't just mentally or emotionally harmful; it's physically harmful. Research has found people with strong social connections live longer, healthier lives than those who are isolated.[120] One study showed that the most isolated individuals were less resilient and three times more likely to die prematurely than those with strong relational ties.[121] Remarkably, this held true even when comparing people with unhealthy habits but strong relationships to those with great health habits but weak social connections. Even though I'm all about healthy habits, I interpret this to mean it's better to eat donuts with good friends than drink kale smoothies alone!

God has placed within each of us what we might call a "human-shaped void." Just as there's a God-shaped void that only He can fill, there's also a space in our hearts that can only be filled by genuine human connection. We can try to fill it with success, achievements, or possessions, but nothing quite fits like authentic relationships.

Mother Teresa, who dedicated her life to serving the poorest of the poor in Kolkata, India, once said, "Loneliness and the feeling of being unwanted is the most terrible poverty."[122] She recognized that even in our crowded cities, many people are dying of loneliness. This emotional and relational poverty can be just as devastating as material poverty.

No Lone Wolves

The first and perhaps biggest obstacle to building resilience is trying to do everything alone. I learned this lesson firsthand. For years, I played sports in high school and worked out vigorously with the encouragement of strength coaches. After high school, I worked out alone but never as consistently and intensely. It wasn't until a few years ago, when I got a trainer who held me accountable, that I started a rigorous weight-training program again. There's something about another person helping you in your journey that makes you better.

The same principle applies to our personal growth, especially pre-trauma. We weren't designed to grow alone. We need others to encourage us, challenge us, and hold us accountable. This way, when crises inevitably come, you have a key to both handling the challenges *and* growing on the other side.

The stakes are high. Sixty-two percent of American leaders know another leader who went through traumatic or high-stress experiences, and they never rebounded to their previous level of performance.[123] Building resilience through quality relationships is key to your sustained success, growth, and wholeness.

Safety in Numbers

Psychological safety is a key benefit of having healthy relationships in place. In 2004, researchers at the National Scientific Council on the Developing Child made an interesting discovery. They learned that, from birth, infants' brains are wired for connection. When adults create psychological safety by responding to an infant's or toddler's needs, the children's brains create neural pathways that support healthy learning and development later in life.[124] This study highlighted what we instinctively know: Human connection isn't just a luxury; it's a necessity for healthy development and thriving. Just as young children need nurture to flourish, we too need meaningful relationships to become all that God designed us to be.

During my season of personal burnout in 2010, a trusted colleague provided me with a safe space for honest conversations without fear of judgment. Over the years, I've intentionally built relationships with friends both within and outside of my immediate church community. One particularly valuable relationship spans over three decades. This friend has journeyed with me from my early faith formation to present day, offering constant wisdom and a feeling of safety and support through life's most challenging moments.

It's not only been my experience, but 71 percent of leaders in America say their key relationships are the greatest factor to their feeling of safety—creating a place of comfort and protecting them from harm.[125]

Your Support Network

So, what are the key relationships we need to build resilience? Decades of experience and research have helped me identify five types of relationships that become a personal "board of advisors": trusted family and friends, mentors, pastors, coaches, and counselors.

Trusted Family and Friends

Relationships are fundamental to our effectiveness in every area of life. As the renowned speaker Zig Ziglar wisely observed, "People who have good relationships at home are more effective in the marketplace."[126] This truth begins with our most intimate relationship, our spouse. In my own journey, my wife has been my life partner, greatest friend, and trusted confidant through every challenge and triumph. I firmly believe our closest friendships should be cultivated with those we know best, our spouse and adult children forming the inner circle of our relational network. These relationships provide the foundation upon which all other connections are built. Some may not find family as a place of safety and support. The good news is, we have the opportunity to develop a close relational network with friends.

A well-rounded network includes two additional types of friends: close friends and affinity friends.

Close friends are those who know and love you. These are the friends who share your values,[127] understand your strengths and weaknesses, and know how to encourage and counsel you most effectively. Close friends are the go-to people when you're feeling isolated or marginalized. They are consistent sources of light and encouragement.

Affinity friends are those who share common interests or similar leadership roles. They are often excellent sounding boards and can help you stay connected to the latest advancements in your field. With respect to challenges and crises, these affinity friends can also share how they overcame similar situations and problems. Affinity friends can help you stay focused and motivated and are a key source of building resilience. And remember, the more resilient we are, the greater our ability to sustainably live and lead from wholeness.

Key Relationship Assessment: Trusted Family and Friends

Here are important questions to help you assess your relationships with family and friends:

- How many close family members and friends do you have who know both your strengths and weaknesses yet still consistently encourage and support you during difficult times?
- When you share a struggle with your closest friends and family members, do you feel heard, understood, accepted, and appropriately challenged?

- How diverse (age, life stage, career, etc.) is your circle of affinity friends who share your professional interests or leadership experiences, and how often do you engage with them?
- In what specific ways have your friendships helped you develop resilience or recover from setbacks in the past year?
- Who is someone you believe would make a valuable close friend that you could reach out to?

Mentors

A mentor is a wise individual who's invested in you and can see your situation from a different perspective. Often, they've taken a similar life path to the one you are now traveling. Due to their years of experience, good mentors will understand the dynamics of your context as well as the necessary resources to help you be successful. Great mentors can also be your biggest cheerleaders. As John Maxwell said, "The true test of relationships is not only how loyal someone is when we fail, but how thrilled they are when we succeed."[128]

It's also helpful to have multiple mentors in different areas of life. No matter where you need guidance in your life and leadership, mentors can point you in the right direction at crucial moments. This direction can make all the difference. For me, a key mentor was a Christian businessman who invested in me while I was in college. During that time, and for years afterward, he provided insights that set me up for long-term success. He taught me how to handle finances, treat employees, and take appropriate entrepreneurial risks.

Key Relationship Assessment: Mentors

Here are important questions to consider in both looking for and assessing key mentors:

- How often do you engage with a mentor who has successfully navigated challenges similar to those you're currently facing?
- When you share vulnerabilities or setbacks with your mentor, how safe do you feel from judgment or criticism?
- In what specific ways has a mentor helped you develop new perspectives or approaches that you wouldn't have considered on your own?
- How balanced is the relationship between receiving encouragement from your mentor and being challenged to grow beyond your comfort zone?
- How consistently does your mentor model the resilience you aspire to develop in your own life?

Pastors

A pastor serves as a spiritual guide who offers both biblical wisdom and practical counsel for life's challenges. As a Christian, I believe pastors play a crucial role in providing perspective that connects our daily experiences to biblical truths and deeper spiritual understanding. Over the years, I've benefited tremendously from personal relationships with the pastors in my life who have helped me navigate difficult seasons with faith and clarity. After my family, no one has provided me with more valuable support and guidance than my pastors.

Interestingly, many people look to leaders and pastors as a source of wisdom, guidance, and insight for major life decisions. Yet these same spiritual leaders often fail to recognize their own need for pastoral care. It's much like a doctor needing a doctor. Even those who shepherd others require shepherding themselves. While pastors readily provide what most people seek (spiritual direction, encouragement, and instruction), they themselves share these same fundamental needs.

The healthiest pastors understand this dynamic and intentionally cultivate relationships where they, too, can receive spiritual guidance and input. This mutual vulnerability creates authentic community and demonstrates that regardless of our role or position, we all need others who can speak truth, offer perspective, and remind us of our core identity and purpose.

Key Relationship Assessment: Pastors

Here are important questions to answer when assessing your relationship with a pastor:

- How frequently do you engage with a pastor or spiritual leader who knows your personal struggles and celebrates your spiritual growth?
- When discussing difficult questions of faith or ethics with your pastor, how comfortable do you feel being completely honest?
- In what specific ways has a pastor helped you connect your everyday challenges to deeper spiritual principles or practices?
- How does your pastor encourage you during difficult times and challenge you to grow in areas of struggle?

- How does your pastor help you live out an authentic spiritual life and integrate into your church community?

Coaches

Another key member of your board of advisors is a life or executive coach. Over the past twenty-five years, coaching has expanded to all levels of successful organizations.[129] A great coach provides clarity, challenge, and care. They help you clarify your purpose, priorities, and vision. They push you to achieve your goals and desired outcomes while offering ongoing support and encouragement. This helps you build resilience and capacity in every area of your life and leadership.

Yet, there's often a big obstacle to receiving coaching. As former World Bank president Jim Yong Kim said, "One of the most important things about leadership is that you have to have the kind of humility that will allow you to be coached."[130] The humility to be coached is vital.

After my season with my first counselor in 2010, it became clear that I needed to employ a leadership coach to help me reintegrate into my professional role. He held me accountable and helped equip me with practical strategies for health, systematic renewal habits, emotional intelligence, and leadership development. This partnership helped me lead more effectively with my team and organization. I intentionally sought out a coach who understood my unique challenges, and I've worked with several great coaches over the years, maintaining an ongoing coaching relationship to this day. These relationships have helped me clarify goals and expectations to prevent regressing into harmful, emotionally draining life and leadership patterns.

Unlike counselors who primarily help you process past and present wounds, coaches work with you in your professional setting. They enhance your emotional intelligence with your team, improve organizational health, and foster professional excellence in your specific leadership context. The coaches I've worked with have helped me set meaningful growth goals that align my daily actions with my deepest values and vision.

Personally, coaching relationships have helped me reach new levels of strength, excellence, and competency. They've advanced both my life and leadership by helping me work more effectively with my team while creating comprehensive life plans. Great coaches ensure you're living in a healthy way across all dimensions—faith, family, finances, fitness, and more—creating alignment between your stated values and your actual behaviors.

The best coaches balance their expertise with a deep understanding of your professional role and personal life. They can also help you develop greater emotional intelligence, enhanced interpersonal relationship strategies, and transformative leadership practices. Effective leadership coaches usually begin by helping you lead yourself well. In turn, this positively influences every facet of your organization.

Key Relationship Assessment: Coaches

Here are important questions to consider in both looking for and assessing a coach:

- Do you have a coach who challenges you to move beyond comfortable patterns and develop new skills or perspectives?

- How effectively does your coach help you recognize blind spots in your leadership approach or personal development journey?
- How clearly have you and your coach defined specific goals and outcomes for your coaching relationship, especially as they relate to building resilience?
- In what ways has your coach helped you improve your self-awareness and emotional intelligence during difficult situations?
- How consistently does your coach provide both supportive encouragement and honest, constructive feedback when you face challenges?

Counselors

Counselors can be a key relationship for regaining healthy soul leadership. They are professionally trained to help you handle past and present emotional wounds in a safe context. They also help you identify unresolved trauma in your life and the corresponding triggers during times of high stress and pressure. Yet, 43 percent of American leaders have not sought professional help for the traumatic experiences or high-stress situations they have experienced.[131] A key relationship with a counselor is a powerful tool for building resilience as they help you unwind the past to fully understand your present circumstances and reactions.

Perhaps the most valuable aspect of a counseling relationship is the safety and confidentiality it provides. It creates a unique environment that allows for emotional transparency, authenticity, and high levels of disclosure that may not be possible in other relationships. In professional leadership settings, it's wise for people in high stress situations to establish a relationship with a qualified professional counselor when possible.

There's transformative power in processing painful experiences because you feel safe enough to voice what is often undisclosed. It's deeply challenging for anyone when they don't have a safe place to process their experiences. Exposing your hurts in therapy lessens their power over you. Safety produces trust. When trust is established, self-disclosure happens naturally, and healing begins to take place.

This is especially true for trauma survivors. If you've experienced abuse or other traumatic situations, you may consider looking for a trauma-informed counselor. From my personal experience, I recommend finding a Christ-centered, professionally trained "trauma-informed therapist" to journey with you through a season of deep healing.

Key Relationship Assessment: Counselors

Here are important questions to consider when evaluating your current counselor or looking for a new one:

- Is the counselor recommended by people you know and trust who have been helped by their professional services?
- Does the counselor have a trauma-informed approach evidenced by additional certifications?
- Does the counselor regularly receive personal counseling, mentorship, and accountability from other professionals?
- Does the counselor readily share their own healing journey?
- Do you connect with this counselor?

- Does your counselor provide a safe, nonjudgmental environment?
- To what extent do you feel your counselor provides both emotional support and practical tools for building resilience?
- What barriers (time, cost, stigma, discomfort) have prevented you from seeking a counseling relationship, and how might you address them?

It's important to note that coaching and counseling services are often seasonal and situational. Also, many counselors operate on sliding-scale fees and take insurance. While I have personally benefited from both coaches and counselors, they can move on and off your board of advisors as you heal and your needs change.

Qualities of Your Board of Advisors

In review, how does your personal board of advisors look? Are you strong in some areas and weaker in others? The most important way you can use this knowledge and your personal assessments is to strengthen your support network. Having identified where your support system needs strengthening, let's examine what to look for in each key relationship.

Your board of advisors becomes an inner circle community, and you are designed to do life in community. Because so much rides on us, we leaders especially need support teams. Each member of your team should have these five qualities: competency, trustworthiness, availability, synchronicity, and contagious vitality. To build the right team, you should examine every person to see if they have these characteristics.[132]

Competency

Overall, you're looking for people who are competent in areas where you are not. It's key to find someone who has demonstrated a track record of excellence and integrity in the areas you want accountability, help, and perspective. Wisdom is vital when choosing advisors as they directly impact your health and well-being and strengthen your resilience.

Trustworthiness

The importance of trustworthiness cannot be overstated.[133] Two components of trustworthiness must be found in each person on your support team. First, everyone has to be able to hold your struggles and needs in confidence. Second, a trustworthy advisor is one who is willing to tell you the truth, even when it's painful. The most trusted advisor is the embodiment of the Stockdale Paradox: "You must never confuse faith that you will prevail in the end—which you can never afford to lose—with the discipline to confront the most brutal facts of your current reality, whatever they might be."[134]

A trustworthy advisor or friend will keep you hopeful about the future while also helping you deal with the tough situations you're facing right now.[135] When you're dealing with a crisis, you want someone who loves you enough to tell you the truth.

Availability

This truth-telling, however, must be paired with consistent presence. Timing matters in crisis support. Regardless of what other qualities a potential friend, mentor, or advisor may have, if that person is emotionally absent when you're in need, then they won't be much help.[136]

A support team only works if you feel comfortable asking for help. If you hold back from approaching support team members because you're worried about bothering them, you miss out on the whole point of having support. Your advisor needs to understand that you might need them at inconvenient times. After all, when do you need people? *When you need people.*

Synchronicity

A good advisor will also have synchronous values and understand your vision and responsibilities as a leader. An advisor with asynchronous values might give advice that sounds smart but leaves you confused and torn between your own beliefs and their conflicting recommendations. For example, a business mentor who values professional accomplishment at any cost will consistently conflict with your desire to prioritize your family.

Contagious Vitality

Finally, an effective support team member will possess contagious vitality, leaving you feeling hopeful and invigorated.[137] Certainly, there will be times when difficult conversations must happen. Yet, a valuable mentor or coach will help you see a path to freedom and victory through the difficulties. Advisors who leave you feeling hopeless, even if they've rightly identified major problems, will prove of little value to you because they only see issues and not solutions. Crises and traumas can leave a leader feeling defeated. Your team of supporters should equip and encourage you.

Developing Your Support Network

A good support team is critical for building resilience and well-being, but you won't get the full benefit unless you create a system for working with them. This means planning how and when you'll communicate with each advisor, and what situations require their input. Your system should fit your life rhythms, and while everyone's approach will be different, effective systems share three key features: simplicity, redundancy, and accountability.

Simplicity

An effective relational network should be simple. If your network is too complicated and takes too much effort to use, you'll quickly abandon it. Leaders rarely have time for complex processes. As your schedule allows, set up regular meetings with everyone on your board of advisors for two important reasons. First, so your advisors stay current with what's happening in your world without needing updates during a crisis. Second, because without regular contact, emotional distance can develop, making it harder for you to be fully open and honest in times of crisis.

Redundancy

A solid support network needs redundancy. Ideally, this means more than one person in each support category. Having multiple advisors gives you more confidence in the advice you receive. Remember what Solomon told us in Proverbs, "in the multitude of counselors there is safety" (11:14 NKJV). It's also practical because when you need immediate help, not everyone will be available. Yet with multiple advisors, you're likely to reach at least one person during a crisis.

Your network should include both people from your daily inner circle and those outside it. People inside your circle are more readily available, while those outside help prevent unhealthy dependency on insiders.

In Exodus 18, Moses's father-in-law, Jethro, who was outside Moses's daily circle but still close to him, gave the wise advice to delegate responsibilities to other capable leaders. Jethro told Moses, "The thing that you do is not good" (v. 17 NKJV). This is called "outside insight." Those within Moses's circle likely couldn't see this solution because they were too close to the situation. Similarly, leaders need outside insight to avoid the "echo chambering" that can happen inside their immediate circle.

Accountability

A good relational network also includes intentional accountability. Your advisors should be able to check in with you to see how you're using their advice. Accountability means being open to both giving and receiving feedback. Without this commitment, relationships can break down due to resentment and resistance. Seeking out these relationships consistently provides the wisdom and support that soul leadership requires.

Building Resilience Through Relationships

As we've explored throughout this chapter, relationships form the essential foundation in our resilience journey. When we build a team of trusted family and friends, mentors, pastors, coaches, and counselors who share our values, we create a support system that helps us through difficult times.

Scripture tells us, "A cord of three strands is not quickly broken" (Ecclesiastes 4:12), reminding us that we are stronger together than we ever could be alone. Leaders who cultivate meaningful relationships have greater resilience, make better decisions, and lead with more wisdom and compassion.

For example, legendary leader Billy Graham wasn't a one-man show. He actually had a tight-knit group of friends and colleagues around him. In fact, they called themselves his "evangelistic band of brothers."[138] These guys had his back in every way. They supported him when times got tough, shielded him from unnecessary drama, and helped him think through big decisions so he could focus on what he did best: communicating and leading.

One of his closest friends T. W. Wilson was Billy's right-hand man for decades. T. W. was the man who made sure Billy's full schedule worked and who provided both security and genuine friendship when Billy needed it most. T. W. kept the constant stream of distractions at bay by helping Billy say "no" to many good opportunities so Billy could focus on what was essential for Billy to accomplish. This inner circle wasn't just about getting things done. They were like a protective wall around his time, energy, and reputation. They made sure he could pour himself into ministry without burning out or getting into compromising situations. Ultimately, they are part of his enduring legacy of integrity, impact, and resilience.

Now, your assessment of your five key relationships—trusted family and friends, mentors, pastors, coaches, and counselors—has likely revealed both strengths and growth opportunities in your support system. Remember that building this team is not a one-time event but an ongoing process. As your leadership journey evolves, so, too, will your needs for support and guidance. Continue to nurture these relationships intentionally with regular connection points and honest exchanges.

Having built a strong team around you, let's look at how taking care of your body also helps you build resilience. Our bodies and minds exist in constant communication, each profoundly affecting the other. This brings us to the second critical component of the resilience equation: physical health. In the next chapter, we'll explore how your physical well-being directly impacts your capacity to handle stress and recover from trauma.

CHAPTER 7

The Resilience Equation: Physical Health

Let's imagine resilience as building a fortress around your life and leadership. In the previous chapter, we established the foundation through relationships, the support system that holds everything together. Now we're moving to the walls and structure of that fortress, the next stage of the resilience equation: your physical health practices. These aren't separate components but interconnected parts of the resilience equation. Just as the strongest buildings need both a solid foundation and sturdy walls, true resilience requires both relational support and physical well-being working together.

As one CEO put it, "Good health is good business."[139] Caring for ourselves is key to stewarding our leadership influence. Remember, the stakes are high, especially for entrepreneurial leaders who set the tone for their entire organization. Healthy leaders heal organizations; hurt leaders hurt organizations.

For leaders, stress is part of the job. Yet what many people miss is how closely our bodies and minds are tied together when it comes to handling that stress. Our mental state can directly influence our physical health. As a study from the Washington University School of Medicine found, the "mind-body connection is built into the brain."[140]

This means if your mental health is suffering, your physical strength will almost always take a hit—and the other way around too. Think of your brain and body as a team: When one side is struggling, the other has to work harder to keep up.

Science proves this true. When we're under constant pressure, our brains and bodies react in ways that can make stress even harder to manage. As we've learned, long-term stress can actually change the structure of your brain, making it tougher to bounce back from setbacks. Research from University of California Berkeley found that chronic stress leads to changes in the brain's white matter, which can disrupt how different parts of your brain communicate and may even set the stage for later mental health problems, like depression or anxiety.[141] Other studies show that people who experience severe or ongoing stress can have a smaller hippocampus, the part of the brain that helps with memory and emotional regulation.[142]

Yet it's not just your brain. Chronic stress throws your hormones out of balance, especially cortisol (the "stress hormone"). When cortisol stays high for too long, it can leave you feeling drained, foggy, overweight, or even physically sick.[143] It can affect everything from your energy and sleep to your immune system and digestion.[144]

This is why focusing on physical health is just as important as focusing on your mental health during stressful times. In this chapter, we'll look at four key areas of physical health:

exercise, nutrition, sleep, and stress management. We'll break each down into a pre-crisis, in-crisis, and post-crisis framework. They all play a role in how well you handle challenges, make decisions, and recover from tough times.

Stress and Trauma in the Body

When we talk about stress and trauma, it's easy to think of them as factors that only affect our minds. But the truth is, stress is a full-body experience. It's not just in your head. It shows up in your muscles, your gut, your heart rate, and even your immune system. That's why building resilience isn't just about mental toughness; it's about preparing your whole body to handle challenges. As a leader, I know firsthand when I'm consistent with positive health habits, there's a direct correlation with how I handle stress and manage crises. Many times after a stressful day just an hour-long walk around my neighborhood both clears my mind and invigorates my body.

Focusing on physical health is just as important as focusing on your mental health during stressful times.

Pre-Crisis: Building a Strong Foundation

Again, think of resilience like a savings account. The healthy habits you build now—before a crisis hits—are like deposits that you'll draw on when times get tough. Research shows that regular exercise, good nutrition, and consistent sleep can actually change how your body reacts to stress, making you more resistant to its harmful effects.[145] For example, people who exercise regularly have lower levels of stress hormones and recover faster after stressful events.[146] Eating a balanced diet[147] and getting enough sleep[148] also help regulate your mood and keep your immune system strong.

In-Crisis: Managing the Body's Response

When a crisis hits—whether it's a high-stakes meeting, a company emergency, or a personal setback—your body goes into "fight, flight, freeze, or fawn" mode.[149] Your heart races, your muscles tense up, and your brain floods your system with stress hormones like cortisol and adrenaline.[150] This is your body's way of helping you respond quickly. Yet if the stress sticks around too long, it can start to do real damage.

Simple physical habits can help you manage this response in the moment. Deep breathing, a short walk, or even a few minutes of stretching can lower your heart rate and help your brain regain focus.[151] Leaders who use these techniques during stressful situations are better able to stay calm, think clearly, and make good decisions.

Post-Crisis: Supporting Recovery

Once the immediate crisis is over, your body needs time to recover. This is when healthy habits are more important than ever. Without them, stress can linger in your system, leading to burnout, sleep problems, or even physical illness.[152] Studies show that people who prioritize rest, nutrition,[153] and gentle movement[154] after a stressful event recover faster and are less likely to develop long-term health problems.

Resilience isn't just about "toughing it out." It's about giving your body the tools it needs to handle stress at every stage—before, during, and after a challenge. You don't have to become a marathon runner or follow an ultra-restrictive diet to benefit from these habits. The goal is to find simple, realistic ways to take care of your body so you're ready for whatever comes your way. After all, it's much easier to build these habits before a crisis hits rather than when you're already overwhelmed.

In the next sections, we'll break down the specific habits that can help you build this kind of whole-body resilience, so you're ready for whatever comes your way.

As we explore these physical dimensions of building resilience, remember, resilience itself isn't our primary goal. Resilience is a means for us to experience *shalom*. Our ultimate aim is to live and lead from wholeness.

Exercise: The Stress Buffer

Most would agree that exercise is good for your body. Paul said, "Physical training is good" (1 Timothy 4:8 NLT). The problem for many leaders is their demanding schedules and complex responsibilities. The incessant travel that frequently accompanies professional roles often undermines the exercise they need to maintain their health. But what many leaders don't realize is that regular exercise is one of the most effective ways to build resilience. Exercise isn't just about athletic performance; it's about training your body and brain to handle pressure.

In the early days, when our church was first growing, I sporadically took time to exercise. It was difficult to balance the constant demands on my time. Interestingly enough, in 2008, prior to my burnout, an injury took me completely out of an exercise rhythm for two years. It's not coincidental that my burnout happened shortly thereafter in 2010. I've noticed, when my physical health is off I neither handle stress well nor make the best decisions. Most leaders will find this to be true. As I've grown as a leader, exercise has become nonnegotiable. It's so important I schedule it on my calendar every week and rarely allow interruptions.

Pre-Crisis: Building Stress Resistance

Think of exercise as your body's way of "stress-proofing" itself. When you make physical activity a regular part of your routine, your body learns to manage stress hormones more efficiently. A study showed that people who exercise regularly are less likely to feel overwhelmed when challenges arise.[155] In fact, even moderate activity—like brisk walking for thirty minutes a few times a week—can make a big difference.[156]

> **Exercise isn't just about athletic performance; it's about training your body and brain to handle pressure.**

Exercise also changes your brain in positive ways. It increases the production of brain chemicals like endorphins and BDNF (brain-derived neurotrophic factor), which help protect against anxiety and depression, and improve memory.[157] This means your brain is better equipped to handle stress when you're physically active. Movement is medicine.

In-Crisis: Managing the Stress Response

When you're in the middle of a crisis, your body goes into high alert. This is when exercise, even in small doses, can help you regain control. Taking a quick walk, doing a few push-ups, or just stretching at your desk can bring your stress levels down.[158]

Post-Crisis: Speeding Up Recovery

Once the stressful event has passed, exercise helps your body recover. Physical activity reduces lingering stress hormones and helps your body return to its normal state faster.[159] Gentle movement can also help you process emotions and sleep better after a tough day.[160]

The bottom line: You don't need to become a gym fanatic (even though there's nothing wrong with that!). Moving your body regularly can make you more resilient, both physically and mentally. Along with going to the gym, one of the other ways this plays out in my life is walking with my wife after work. We get sunshine, fresh air, and process the day with each other.

When you walk, the rhythmic left-right movement of your body naturally engages both hemispheres of your brain through a process called alternating bilateral stimulation.[161] This kind of stimulation—similar to what occurs in therapies like eye movement desensitization and reprocessing (EMDR)[162]—can help the brain process emotions and experiences more effectively. When walking is paired with positive, emotionally attuned conversation, it further activates the brain's emotional and relational centers, provides a form of trauma therapy, and promotes safety and well-being. Research suggests that this combination of movement and relational engagement can reduce stress, foster emotional regulation, and support trauma recovery. In essence, walking and talking together can serve as a simple, God-given form of embodied healing.

Exercise Assessment

- How often do you make time for exercise despite your busy schedule?
- Have you noticed a connection between your physical activity levels and your ability to handle stress?
- What happens to your exercise routine when you face a crisis or an extremely busy period?
- Do you have an exercise plan when you travel?
- What one small change could you make this week to improve your physical health and resilience?

Nutrition: The Way You Eat Under Pressure

What you eat is about more than fueling your body. It's also about supporting your brain, especially when you're under stress. The right nutrition can help you stay calm, think clearly, and recover faster from tough situations. For leaders, building resilience means paying attention to food choices every day.

Over the last few years, I've had to learn new eating habits. My routine now includes a simple breakfast of some form of protein and a cup of coffee, trying to avoid processed sugar at lunch in favor of whole foods, and eating dinner earlier in the evening. These small changes have made a noticeable difference in my resilience and clarity—although I allow myself to cheat a little on the weekends!

Pre-Crisis: Building a Resilient Body and Brain

Eating well on a regular basis sets you up for success when challenges come your way. Diets rich in fruits, vegetables, lean proteins, and healthy fats support your immune system and help regulate your mood.[163] For example, research shows that people who eat a Mediterranean-style diet (lots of vegetables, nuts, fish, and olive oil) have lower rates of depression and anxiety.[164] Omega-3 fatty acids, found in fish and some plant sources, can even improve your body's stress response.[165] Additionally, a high-quality multivitamin can improve mood and help you feel better.[166]

In-Crisis: Making Smart Choices Under Pressure

When you're stressed, it's tempting to reach for sugary snacks, excess caffeine, or comfort foods. But these can actually make things worse by causing energy crashes and mood swings.[167] Instead, try to choose foods that keep your blood sugar steady. Staying hydrated is just as important; even mild dehydration can affect your focus and decision-making.[168] Years ago, I was losing my voice and was unsure why. As a pastor and communicator, my voice is essential to my career and livelihood. After seeing doctors across my region, it came down to one simple fact: I was dehydrated and it was affecting my vocal cords. The solution: Drink more water, Steve!

If you know a tough day is coming, plan ahead. Pack a healthy snack or meal (along with your water bottle) so you're not stuck with only unhealthy options. This small step can make a big difference in how you feel and perform.

Post-Crisis: Supporting Recovery and Repair

After a stressful event, your body needs nutrients to recover. Protein helps repair muscles and tissues, while complex carbohydrates help restore your energy.[169] Vitamins and minerals from fruits and vegetables support your immune system, which can get run down after prolonged stress.[170]

Here's our resilience takeaway: Eating well isn't about perfection, strict diets, or just looking good. It's about making small, smart choices that help your body and brain stay strong and handle stress better.

Nutrition Assessment

- How do your eating patterns change when you're under stress or facing a crisis?
- Do you notice a connection between what you eat and your ability to think clearly during challenging situations?
- How often do you plan ahead for healthy meals when you know you'll have a demanding day?
- How consistent are you with staying hydrated throughout your workday?
- What small change could you make to your nutrition habits this week to support your resilience?

Sleep: The Great Cognitive Reset

Sleep is often the first thing busy leaders sacrifice, but it's actually one of your strongest tools for building resilience. Good sleep is about giving your brain and body a chance to reset, repair, and prepare for whatever comes next.

Prioritizing consistent, high-quality sleep is another deposit in your resilience bank. People who regularly get enough sleep have better emotional control, stronger immune systems, and sharper thinking skills.[171] In fact, the Division of Sleep Medicine at Harvard Medical School found just one week of poor sleep can make you more sensitive to stress and less able to manage your emotions.[172] For leaders, just one moment of emotional dysregulation can cost you greatly—don't forget Moses!

Pre-Crisis: Building a Sleep Routine

How often have you heard a leader say they only need a few hours of sleep per night? But getting the right amount of sleep in the right environment allows your brain to "defragment its hard drive." Sleep is restorative and helps your brain and body return to an optimal state of health. Experts recommend aiming for seven to nine hours of sleep each night and keeping a consistent sleep schedule, even on weekends.[173] I used to stay up until midnight reading and researching, and before my burnout, I was emailing and texting late into the night. One thing I'm trying to implement right now is being in bed by 9:30, which allows me to get up early, fresh and ready for the day.

In-Crisis: Protecting Your Rest

When you're in the middle of a crisis, it's tempting to stay up late working or worrying. But this is when your body and brain need sleep the most. Sleep helps you process emotions, solve problems, and make better decisions under pressure.[174]

If you can't get a full night's sleep, even a short nap (twenty to thirty minutes) can help improve alertness and mood.[175] Try to keep your sleep environment calm and dark and avoid screens before bed, as blue light can disrupt your natural sleep cycle.[176]

Post-Crisis: Using Sleep to Recover

After a stressful event, your body needs extra rest to recover and repair. Research shows that sleep helps clear out stress hormones, restore your immune system, and rebuild your emotional reserves.[177] A study at Washington State University's Elson S. Floyd College of Medicine found that, "Increasing the amount of time spent asleep immediately after a traumatic experience may ease any negative consequences."[178]

Adequate sleep is a necessity for leaders who want to stay resilient. Protecting your sleep before, during, and after stressful times will help you handle challenges with a clear mind and a steady hand.

Sleep Assessment

- How consistent is your sleep schedule throughout the week?
- What happens to your sleep habits during times of crisis or high stress?
- How often do you sacrifice sleep to get more work done?
- Do you notice a connection between your sleep quality and your ability to handle stress and make good decisions?
- What one change could you make to improve your sleep routine this week?

Stress Management: Techniques for Building Real-Time Resilience

No matter how healthy your habits are, stress will still show up—especially in leadership roles. The key is learning how to manage it in real time, so it doesn't build up and take a toll on your mind or body. Stress management isn't just about "calming down." It's about giving yourself practical ways to stay focused, clear-headed, and resilient.

Pre-Crisis: Practicing Stress-Reduction Habits

Building stress management into your routine before a crisis hits gives you tools to draw on when you need them most. Techniques such as meditation (especially biblical meditation and prayer), deep breathing, and progressive muscle relaxation have all been shown to lower baseline stress levels and improve emotional regulation.[179] Even just a few minutes a day can make a difference. People who practice these skills regularly are better prepared to stay calm and focused when challenges arise.[180] These exercises are akin to ancient Christian monastic techniques practiced for millennia. Regarding meditation's physical effects, renowned Christian author Richard Foster said, "The aim is to center the attention of the body, the emotions, the mind, and the spirit upon 'the glory of God in the face of Christ (2 Cor. 4:6).'" He went on to say, "If inwardly we are fraught with distractions and anxiety, a consciously chosen posture of peace and relaxation will have a tendency to calm our inner turmoil."[181]

In-Crisis: Using Real-Time Tools

When you're in the thick of a crisis, your body's stress response can make it hard to think clearly. Simple, evidence-based techniques can help you regain control in the moment. For example, tactical breathing (also called box breathing or the 4-4-4-4 method) can quickly lower your heart rate and help your brain shift out of fight, flight, or freeze mode.[182]

Box breathing involves four simple steps: Inhale for four seconds, hold for four seconds, exhale for four seconds, and hold again for four seconds before repeating. This technique has been adopted by Navy SEALs to maintain calm and focus during high-pressure situations. It's also used by first responders, professional athletes, and healthcare workers to manage stress in critical moments. Research shows it effectively activates the parasympathetic nervous system, reducing anxiety and improving cognitive function when you need it most.[183]

Post-Crisis: Processing and Releasing Tension

Once the immediate stress is over, it's important to help your body and brain return to baseline. This might mean taking a few minutes to sit quietly, go for a walk, or stretch.[184] Research shows that people who actively process and release stress are less likely to carry it forward, reducing their risk of burnout and long-term health problems.[185]

Stress management isn't about avoiding stress. It's about having a toolkit of strategies you can use at any time. By consistently practicing these techniques, you can keep stress from building up and protect your resilience for the long haul.

Stress Management Assessment

- What stress management techniques do you practice regularly?
- Have you considered adopting prayer rituals as a way to calm and ground yourself?
- How confident are you in your ability to use real-time tools (like box breathing) when you're in a high-pressure situation?
- After experiencing a stressful event, what specific actions do you take to help your body and mind recover?

- How intentional are you about processing stress rather than carrying it forward?
- What one stress management technique could you begin practicing this week?

Building Resilience Through Physical Health

The connection between physical health and leadership resilience is undeniable. Throughout this chapter, we've seen how exercise serves as a stress buffer, nutrition fuels both mind and body, sleep resets our cognitive capacity, and stress management techniques provide real-time tools for maintaining balance. These aren't merely "nice-to-haves." Instead, they're essential components of sustainable soul leadership.

Consider the pastor facing a challenging project who relies on morning routines like exercise or biblical meditation and prayer to maintain the mental clarity needed for complex decisions. Or the leader navigating difficult employee issues who finds that proper nutrition and adequate sleep dramatically improve her conflict resolution abilities. Even the executive facing market volatility discovers that regular stress management practices keep him from making reactive decisions that could damage long-term outcomes.

Remember that building resilience is like constructing a fortress. First, we established relationships as the foundation. Now, we've built the walls and structure through physical health practices. Both elements work together, providing the strength and stability needed to withstand life's inevitable hardships.

The research is clear: Leaders who neglect their physical well-being are more vulnerable to burnout, poor decision-making, and diminished effectiveness. Conversely, those who integrate this chapter's four key practices into their lives demonstrate increased resilience. Their bodies and brains work as allies rather than adversaries in the face of challenges.

Small, consistent actions build powerful habits over time.

Start small. Choose one area where you can make an immediate improvement. Perhaps it's establishing a consistent sleep schedule, adding a short daily walk, planning nutrient-rich meals, or practicing five minutes of tactical breathing. Small, consistent actions build powerful habits over time.

While physical practices form an essential component of resilience, they are not the complete picture. The strongest leaders recognize that true resilience also requires internal work—the cultivation of mental, emotional, and spiritual practices that nourish the soul and clarify purpose.

CHAPTER 8

The Resilience Equation: Spiritual, Mental, and Emotional

Building resilience isn't complete without addressing what happens in our hearts and minds—the inner world that ultimately determines how we interpret and respond to life's challenges. This final piece of the resilience equation explores the spiritual, mental, and emotional practices that help leaders stay strong from the inside out. When these three dimensions work together, they create an internal fortitude that can withstand even the most severe challenges of life and leadership.

You can think of resilience as building a fortress around your life and leadership. In previous chapters, we established the foundation through relationships and constructed sturdy walls through physical health practices. Now we're focusing on the heart of the fortress, the inner resources that give purpose and direction to everything else.

Spiritual practices connect us to something—yes, *Someone*—greater than ourselves, providing purpose and perspective during difficult times. Mental disciplines shape how we interpret challenges, helping us maintain clarity and focus when pressure mounts. Emotional habits determine how we process feelings in healthy ways, neither suppressing them nor being overwhelmed by them.

Leaders who neglect these inner dimensions often find themselves making decisions based on fear rather than wisdom, reacting from emotion instead of responding with purpose, and ultimately, burning out even when they appear successful. The consequences impact not only their leadership effectiveness but also their personal lives, relationships, and the health of their organizations.

At the heart of maintaining these inner dimensions is what leadership coach and author Greg Salciccioli calls "systematic renewal." He explains it like this: "Systematic renewal is the powerful process by which we engage in replenishing activities to continually recover the energy we're consuming."[186] This concept provides the perfect framework for understanding how leaders stay resilient over the long term. Our study found that past trauma drives over one-third of leaders to exhaustion and burnout.[187] Without these replenishing activities, the toll is serious.

Think about it like this: In life and leadership, your batteries get drained. The reason you charge your phone is because you use it. Similarly, leaders need to recharge because they get drained and need reserves on board to handle unexpected challenges.

In today's world of electric vehicles, we've become increasingly familiar with the importance of recharging stations. Your leadership journey requires the same intentional approach to recharging. These are refueling opportunities that provide the energy you need to accomplish your mission. When your soul is healthy and your brain is integrated, you have the energy needed for sustained, effective leadership through both calm and turbulent seasons.

Leaders who cultivate healthy spiritual, mental, and emotional practices demonstrate better decision-making under pressure, recover more quickly from setbacks, and better sustain their leadership impact over the long term.[188] They're able to transform challenges into opportunities for growth.

In the pages ahead, we'll examine how daily spiritual rhythms, mental disciplines, and emotional awareness work together to create what the book of Daniel calls "an excellent spirit" (6:3 NKJV), a quality that enables leaders to succeed even in the most challenging circumstances. To illustrate how this practice of systematic renewal works in real life, let's look at one of history's most resilient leaders.

From Exile to Excellence

Imagine being fifteen years old when enemy soldiers storm your city. Within days, you're torn from everything familiar—family, friends, culture, language—and forced to march roughly 800 grueling miles to a foreign capital. This wasn't a chapter in some dystopian novel. This was Daniel's reality in 605 BC.

The dust of Jerusalem had barely settled on his sandals when Babylonian officials changed his name from Daniel, meaning "God is my judge," to Belteshazzar, which is "prince of Bel," the patron god of Babylonian king Nebuchadnezzar (Daniel 1:7). This was the first step in an aggressive campaign to erase his identity. The message was clear: Forget who you were. Forget your God. You belong to Babylon now.

From his earliest days, Daniel had established regular practices of connecting with God—habits that would serve as his anchor through decades of crisis. These weren't merely religious rituals but systematic renewal practices that replenished his spiritual, mental, and emotional reserves. Even as a young man, Daniel understood what many leaders discover too late: Resilience must be built before it's needed.

For many young captives, this traumatic beginning would have defined their entire story. Yet Daniel not only survived, he thrived. What transformed this terrified teenager into one of history's most influential leaders?

Even as a young man, Daniel understood what many leaders discover too late: Resilience must be built before it's needed.

Consider Daniel's first test. The royal officials presented him with delicacies from the king's table—foods that violated his deepest religious convictions. It would not have been difficult to justify compliance: "I'm a captive. I have no choice. God will understand." Instead, Daniel proposed a daring alternative: "Test your servants for ten days: Give us nothing but vegetables to eat and water to drink" (Daniel 1:12). It was a creative solution that honored both his captors and his convictions.

Then came the night that changed everything. King Nebuchadnezzar bolted upright in his bed, shaken by a nightmare he couldn't understand or ignore. His demand was as irrational as it was deadly: Interpret a dream he refused to describe or die along with all the court advisors. While Babylon's wise men protested the impossibility, Daniel requested time and gathered three friends for an urgent prayer session. Then he stood before the most powerful man on earth with extraordinary clarity: "No wise man, enchanter, magician or diviner can explain to the king the mystery he has asked about, but there is a God in heaven who reveals mysteries" (Daniel 2:27–28).

The king's astonished face told Daniel everything—he'd nailed it. Not just the dream's content but its meaning. Filled with gratitude, the king promoted Daniel to rule "over the entire province of Babylon and placed him in charge of all its wise men" (Daniel 2:48). This was more than an advisory role. Daniel became the equivalent of a prime minister, second only to the king himself in the most powerful empire on earth. After receiving this remarkable promotion, instead of simply basking in his success, Daniel immediately secured positions for his friends (Daniel 2:49). Even in triumph, he maintained his connections.

This integration of spirit, mind, and emotion didn't make Daniel crisis-proof; it made him crisis-ready.

Daniel then weathered the fall of Babylon to the Persians in 539 BC, a political earthquake that destroyed countless lives. Yet his resilient spirit so impressed the Persian king that jealous officials had to create a special trap. They knew Daniel's only vulnerability was his unwavering spiritual rhythm and practice of prayer. When they outlawed prayer, Daniel simply continued his discipline. "Now when Daniel knew that the writing was signed, he went home. And in his upper room, with his windows open toward Jerusalem, he knelt down on his knees three times that day, and prayed and gave thanks before his God, as was his custom since early days" (Daniel 6:10 NKJV).

This was Daniel's systematic renewal practice, his regular refueling that kept him connected to God and gave him the strength he needed for his demanding leadership role. Three times daily, he disconnected from the pressures of leadership to reconnect with his source of wisdom and power. This consistent practice built reserves that carried him through crisis after crisis without collapsing under the weight of trauma that would have destroyed others.

Throughout his life—even facing the lions' den—Daniel maintained his emotional equilibrium. The text offers no dramatic scenes of Daniel weeping or raging against his fate. Instead, we see the quiet confidence of a man whose spiritual practices had prepared him for this moment.

What fueled this extraordinary resilience? Scripture describes Daniel as having "an excellent spirit" (Daniel 5:12 NKJV). Here, the original word means "extraordinary" or "exceeding," indicating he possessed exceptional capacity and well-developed leadership abilities.[189] This wasn't mere personality or willpower. The narrative makes clear that Daniel's connection with God was his true source of resolve. It was a wellspring that nourished his mental clarity and emotional stability through decades of crisis.

Each morning, Daniel took time to pray. Every challenge, he processed through the lens of divine perspective. He navigated through relational issues with emotional intelligence grounded in spiritual wisdom. The integration of spiritual practices created an internal fortitude that carried him through nearly seventy years of high-level leadership positions across two world empires.

For today's leaders facing their own lions' dens—corporate takeovers, organizational crises, financial collapses, relational fallouts, personal attacks—Daniel's journey offers more than ancient history. It provides a blueprint for building resilience from the inside out, where spiritual practices strengthen mental clarity, mental disciplines regulate emotional responses, and emotional intelligence deepens relational connection.

This integration of spirit, mind, and emotion didn't make Daniel crisis-proof; it made him crisis-ready. Because he had these core disciplines and built resilience, crises that could have produced traumatic responses in his brain and body instead became opportunities for him to demonstrate wisdom and courage. He consistently navigated through adversity without being diminished by it. That same resilience is available to you and any leader willing to develop these inner practices.

Your Spiritual Recharging Plan

Daniel's extraordinary journey reveals something profound about resilience: It's not a quality we're simply born with; we build resilience through consistent practices and habits. Daniel didn't develop his excellent, extraordinary spirit overnight. It was forged through daily disciplines that connected him to God even in the most challenging times.

For leaders, the question isn't whether we'll face crises; it's whether we'll have developed the inner resources to navigate them with wisdom and grace when they arrive. As Daniel's example shows us, the time to build resilience is long before we need it.

How do we develop this kind of resilience in our own life and leadership? The answer begins with intentionality—creating a systematic spiritual plan that provides the resources for mental clarity and emotional stability.

As with our human relationships, our connection with God requires commitment to grow. We need a spiritual plan that serves as a consistent recharging station for our leadership journey. While physical and mental health plans vary by individual, spiritual health plans share common elements despite their personal nature.

Think about what makes your closest human relationships work. All healthy relationships require both listening and talking. They demand quality time together, including those special moments when you focus exclusively on each other. Close relationships often involve shared activities like working, serving, and enjoying life together.

To develop these same elements in our relationship with God, Scripture points us toward specific spiritual practices: prayer and Bible study. These foundational disciplines create the framework where genuine connection with God can flourish. Many leaders have noted over the years that their daily time spent reading God's Word has strengthened their leadership. As philanthropist and founder of Hobby Lobby, David Green, said, "Run your business in harmony with God's laws. Seek to please God in everything you do."[190] I've heard Mr. Green speak many times, and his daily engagement with the Bible is a recurring theme.

Recharging Activity: Connecting with God for Leadership Resilience

Let's talk about how to actually connect with God day to day through prayer and reading Scripture. Prayer is simple:

It's just you talking to God while also making space to listen. When you read the Bible daily, you begin to understand God's will and also receive specific guidance for your current challenges.

Abraham Lincoln, whose leadership was tested through America's greatest crisis, understood the power of this connection: "I have been driven many times upon my knees by the overwhelming conviction that I had nowhere else to go. My own wisdom and that of all about me seemed insufficient for that day."[191] This was a systematic renewal practice that fueled his resilience during the nation's darkest hours.

Research consistently demonstrates the mental health benefits of prayer and meditation.[192] A study published in the *Journal of Behavioral Medicine* found that spiritual meditation led to greater decreases in anxiety and stress compared to nonreligious meditation.[193] Dr. Andrew Newberg's brain imaging studies at Thomas Jefferson University show that prayer activates regions of the brain associated with focus and attention while decreasing activity in areas linked to anxiety and stress.[194]

As Wayne Cordeiro describes in his book *Leading on Empty*, the spiritual practices of Bible engagement, prayer, and meditation serve as essential recharging stations for leaders. After experiencing his own burnout at age 52, Cordeiro discovered it was his daily disciplines of connecting with God that had been his "true north" all along. For instance, it was his daily habit of prayer and Scripture reading that kept him anchored when everything else was spinning out of control. When his serotonin levels were depleted and his system was shutting down, his time with God was one of the key elements that helped him recover.

One of the biggest challenges you face as a leader is the constant demand on your time. It's tempting to cut back on spiritual habits when wyou're busy, but this ultimately damages both your relationship with God and your leadership effectiveness.

Don't worry that a daily routine will make your time with God feel stale or boring. Actually, the opposite happens. You're creating space for the Holy Spirit to restore and renew you. You'll discover that God brings fresh insights and energy to each new day.

One particularly helpful spiritual practice is journaling.[195] When you reflect and journal during your time with God, it helps you focus your thoughts and truly hear what God is saying to you. Making time to reflect is not just a spiritual practice but an essential leadership habit in gaining wisdom, perspective, and insight. Later, you can look back through your journal entries to see how God has guided your growth and answered your prayers over time.

These spiritual recharging practices aren't about checking boxes; they're fuel for your leadership mission. They provide the wisdom, perspective, and inner strength needed to navigate the complexities of leadership with clarity and purpose. Your systematic spiritual renewal habits directly impact your leadership effectiveness.

Recharging Activity: Mental Practices for Leadership Resilience

While spiritual practices establish our connection with God, mental disciplines shape how we interpret and respond to leadership challenges. Here again, Scripture offers a powerful model in the life of Joshua—another leader who faced extraordinary pressure.

Remember Moses, who led Israel through the wilderness but did not enter the promised land? His protégé, Joshua, was tasked with the monumental challenge of leading a once traumatized nation into hostile territory. Talk about pressure! When we first meet Joshua, he is Moses's assistant. By the end of his story, he is leading Israel to possess the land promised to Abraham centuries earlier.

What transformed this assistant into one of history's most successful national and military leaders? What mental framework allowed him to succeed? The answer is found in God's instructions to Joshua at this critical leadership transition:

> This Book of the Law shall not depart from your mouth, but you shall meditate in it day and night, that you may observe to do according to all that is written in it. For then you will make your way prosperous, and then you will have good success (Joshua 1:8 NKJV).

This verse demonstrates the core of mental resilience, a framework I call "reject, receive, act."

Reject

Joshua had to reject negative voices and limiting beliefs. Years earlier, ten of the twelve spies Moses sent to explore Canaan returned with a fearful report declaring, "We can't attack those people; they are stronger than we are" (Numbers 13:31). Joshua had to consciously filter out these voices of fear and doubt. Similarly, leaders must identify and reject toxic inputs that drain mental energy and distort perspective.

Receive

Joshua was instructed to meditate on God's Word day and night. The Hebrew concept of meditation isn't passive contemplation—it means to mutter, to speak, to actively engage with truth. Over the years, I've found it helpful to consistently speak God's truth over my life. This is called biblical meditation and is an integral part of what psychologists call positive self-talk.

When we actively speak God's truth over our lives, we encourage ourselves spiritually *and* rewire our brains, empowering us to respond more effectively to life's challenges.

David practiced this when he said, "Why, my soul, are you downcast? Why so disturbed within me? Put your hope in God, for I will yet praise him, my Savior and my God" (Psalm 42:5). He spoke directly to his soul's condition, encouraging himself to put his hope in God. Researchers discovered that positive affirmations activate specific brain areas related to self-awareness and personal value, enhancing the capacity to face challenges and change behaviors.[196] In other words, when we actively speak God's truth over our lives, we encourage ourselves spiritually *and* rewire our brains, empowering us to respond more effectively to life's challenges.

Joshua intentionally filled his mind with God's promises and perspective and declared them. For today's leaders, this means consciously choosing what information, concepts, and beliefs you'll accept as programming for your mental software.

Act

Notice God didn't just tell Joshua to think about the law, but "to do according to all that is written in it" (Joshua 1:8 NKJV). Mental resilience is incomplete without action. Joshua had to translate beliefs into behavior, faith into forward movement. When leaders act on what they speak and believe, they strengthen neural pathways that build resilience.[197] The book of Joshua depicts a leader who acted decisively, overcame great odds, and led consistently throughout his life. This is demonstrated by Joshua leading three successful military campaigns to conquer the promised land against fierce opposition. His success directly resulted from his regular habit of meditating on God's Word.

Programming Resilience

> **Mental resilience is incomplete without action.**

This mental framework addresses a fundamental truth about leadership resilience: Your mind needs to be systematically renewed just as much as your spirit. Remember, like a computer that needs new programming, your brain has remarkable neuroplasticity—the ability to rewire itself based on what you consistently think and do.

As psychiatrist and author Dr. Norman Doidge noted, "Each thought alters the physical state of your brain synapses at a microscopic level."[198] This scientific insight perfectly aligns with what Scripture has always taught: "Be transformed by the renewing of your mind" (Romans 12:2).

Think about King Saul, whom we discussed earlier. His mental programming was established early when his father didn't fully trust him. When he went to find the lost donkeys, his father sent servants with him. This was a subtle message that Saul couldn't handle responsibility alone. This early programming created a belief system where Saul doubted his capabilities.

That's why we see Saul hiding in the luggage when he was called to be king—not out of humility, but out of insecurity. He was experiencing what is often called impostor syndrome, which means being in a position of leadership but feeling unworthy and incompetent, constantly afraid of being found out.[199] This unhealthy belief system eventually led to his downfall.

Building mental resilience requires attention to three key areas, which help us put the "reject, receive, act" framework into practice.

What are you taking in? Be strategic about your information diet. Just as you're careful about what food you put in your body, be discerning about what information you allow into your mind. News, social media, books, podcasts, and conversations all program your mental software. Choose inputs that strengthen rather than deplete you. As best-selling author James Clear put it, "The information you consume each day is the soil from which your future thoughts grow."[200]

What are you filtering out? Not all information deserves your attention. Learning to recognize and reject toxic inputs—whether negative news, unhelpful criticism, or your own catastrophic thinking—is essential for building mental resilience. As the great Stoic philosopher and Roman emperor Marcus Aurelius said, "You have power over your mind—not outside events. Realize this, and you will find strength."[201]

What are you acting on? Mental resilience helps us translate beliefs into action. When you consistently act on what you believe, you strengthen both your confidence and your competence. Every time you successfully navigate something difficult, you're literally rewiring your brain to be more resilient.

These mental disciplines form the programming of your leadership mind—the operating system that determines how you process challenges and opportunities. When properly maintained, this mental framework becomes a powerful recharging station that builds your capacity to handle adversity.

According to a study from Claremont Graduate University, leaders with strong mental resilience demonstrate several key qualities:

1. **Belief system management:** They consistently evaluate and adjust their core beliefs about themselves, others, and their circumstances.[202]
2. **Thought discipline:** They recognize unhealthy thought patterns and intentionally redirect their thinking toward truth and possibility.[203]
3. **Cognitive flexibility:** They can adapt their thinking to changing circumstances without being rigidly attached to one approach.[204]
4. **Mental toughness:** They've developed the capacity to persist through difficulty because they believe "I can do hard things."
5. **Action orientation:** They break through paralysis and passivity by taking decisive action based on their beliefs.[205]

Just like Joshua constantly meditated on Scripture, your mental disciplines need consistent attention. When you establish these practices before crises hit, you're building reserves that will carry you through leadership challenges that would otherwise produce extreme traumatic responses. These mental disciplines protect your brain from the damaging effects of chronic stress, leadership pressure, and trauma.

Recharging Activity: Emotional Practices for Leadership Resilience

While spiritual connections and mental disciplines are vital, leaders often underestimate the importance of emotional resilience. Your emotional health directly impacts your decision-making, relationships, and overall leadership effectiveness. Let's explore the key recharging activities that build emotional reserves.

The Science of Emotional Recharging

Understanding the biological basis of emotional depletion helps us appreciate why systematic renewal is so critical. When you go throughout your week, you're constantly drawing on key neurochemical resources:

- *Serotonin* regulates mood, sleep, and feelings of well-being.[206]
- *Endorphins* provide natural pain relief and feelings of pleasure.[207]
- *Dopamine* drives motivation and reward feelings.[208]
- *Adrenaline* activates your body's fight-or-flight response.[209]

As leadership demands increase, your serotonin and endorphin levels become gradually depleted. When this happens, your body increasingly relies on adrenaline to keep you functioning, essentially operating in an emergency mode that was never designed for long-term use.[210]

This is why emotional recharging is biologically necessary for leaders. The following practices aren't merely nice suggestions; they're essential activities that replenish your emotional reserves and prevent the physiological collapse that damages too many leadership journeys.

Emotional Recharging Activity: Managing Emotional Energy

Every leader knows the feeling of being stretched too thin. You're continually saying "yes" to good opportunities, yet your soul runs on empty. That's because leadership isn't about time management alone; it's about energy management.

Every "yes" costs you something, drawing from your emotional reserves. While leaders are responsible for serving others, that doesn't mean we need to say "yes" to everything. Every time you say "yes" to one thing, you're saying "no" to something else—and sometimes that's the health of your soul.

For leaders, needing to be needed can be a powerful motivator, but it's also a setup for emotional depletion. Leaders are wired to lift, build, and solve problems. Yet when that drive goes unchecked, it quickly drains the soul and moves us into dangerous territory. The constant push to meet needs and fix problems creates an illusion of vitality that feels productive but is unsustainable. Without boundaries to safeguard the health of our souls, leaders eventually run on fumes. Research shows that chronic output without recovery leads to emotional exhaustion and burnout.[211]

Even Jesus modeled healthy boundaries. After a full day of ministry, He withdrew to pray (Mark 1:35–37 NKJV). When the disciples found Him and said, "Everyone is looking for You," He didn't rush back to meet every demand. He stayed focused on His mission. Sometimes the most important thing you can do is say "no."

Learning to say "no" gracefully is a vital skill in managing emotional energy and maintaining relationships.

As your influence grows, so do expectations and opportunities that sometimes exceed your capacity. Learning to say "no" gracefully is a vital skill in managing emotional energy and maintaining relationships. Saying "no" to some opportunities isn't selfish; it's effective soul leadership. It's stewardship of your emotional energy so you can serve from a place of overflow, not depletion. A gracious "no" might sound like this: "Thank you for the opportunity. I'm honored you asked, but given my current responsibilities, I'm unable to say yes at this time." It's kind, clear, and emotionally freeing.

Here are two practical ways to manage emotional energy:

- Conduct an "Energy Audit": Review your major commitments each week, month, and year. Note which ones filled you or drained you. Ask yourself, What do I need to say "no" to so I can say "yes" to what's most important?

- Schedule Margin: Just as you block time for meetings, block time for emotional recharging activities. Protect it like a major appointment.

Energy is one of the most valuable resources for a leader. Soul leadership means managing your energy with wisdom, protecting your peace, and saying "no" when necessary so you can say "yes" to what matters most.

Emotional Recharging Activity: Gratitude

Recent research has shown that over time, gratitude leads to greater social support and a reduction in levels of stress and depression.[212] Ancient wisdom agrees. The Bible prescribed gratitude as a necessary ingredient for living in peace and maintaining a healthy soul. Philippians 4:6–7 says, "Do not be anxious about anything, but in every situation, by prayer and petition, with thanksgiving, present your requests to God. And the peace of God, which transcends all understanding, will guard your hearts and your minds in Christ Jesus." Interestingly, the New Testament writer Paul was in prison when he penned this letter to the church at Philippi. Gratitude is a time-tested buffer against the impacts of trauma, stress, and adversity.

Another study suggests that both those with higher and lower levels of natural resilience increased in resilience when they focused on gratitude.[213] Here's what's fascinating—the key is not experiencing great circumstances; the key is choosing gratitude. Research shows that favorable circumstances do not increase gratitude or resilience.[214] When we start with gratitude, we build the resilience that helps sustain us through difficult circumstances.

Here are two practical ways to cultivate gratitude. One is keeping a gratitude journal by writing down what you're thankful for each day and verbally reciting what you've written. A second is going on a "gratitude walk," a practice my friend Jon Gordon describes as intentionally walking while again speaking aloud what you're grateful for.[215] Over time, these habits don't just change your perspective in the moment—they reprogram your brain to have a hopeful, positive outlook even when facing difficult circumstances.

Emotional Recharging Activity: The Power of Sabbath

Among the Ten Commandments, "Remember the Sabbath day by keeping it holy" (Exodus 20:8) stands out as a practice with profound implications for building emotional resilience as a leader. Beyond a religious to-do, it's a powerful emotional recharging station built into the rhythm of creation itself.

Think about this: God didn't rest on the seventh day of creation because He was tired. He ceased creating and rested to set an example for us. As theologian Walter Brueggemann said, "God is not a workaholic."[216] Even before sin entered the world, humans were designed for consistent periods of rest, replenishment, and renewal. I'm not suggesting you must follow the specific Old Testament pattern of sundown Friday to sundown Saturday. What matters is that you, like every leader, need a consistent twenty-four-hour period of downtime and emotional replenishment each week. Yes, even you!

Humanity's first full day on earth wasn't spent working but resting!

As Peter Scazzero put it in *The Emotionally Healthy Leader*, "Biblical Sabbath is a twenty-four-hour block of time, in which we stop work, enjoy rest, practice delight, and contemplate God."[217] Sabbath is a reset button for your soul—it recenters you around what matters most: God, family, relationships, and renewal.

Our modern approach to work completely contradicts this design. In Western culture, we celebrate those who work nonstop, taking pride in being constantly available and rarely taking breaks. We think the most "dedicated" leaders never truly disconnect. But look at creation. Adam and Eve were both created during the sixth day, and the seventh was the day of Sabbath. Humanity's first full day on earth wasn't spent working but resting! We weren't designed to work until exhaustion and then rest. We were designed to work *from* a place of rest.

Scazzero noted the divine rhythm for humans is Sabbath-work–Sabbath-work, not work-work-work-collapse–more work.[218] This Sabbath rhythm offers physiological benefits such as increased energy levels, emotional renewal, increased mental acuity, and higher levels of productivity. God knows how we tick best! Regular Sabbath rest allows your neurochemical systems to rebalance: serotonin levels rise, endorphins replenish, and overtaxed adrenal glands recover.[219] It's like pushing the reset button on your emotional operating system.

The Sabbath also resets the pace of your life. In our hyper-accelerated culture, we're constantly traveling too fast. The weekly Sabbath serves as a regular calibration point that ensures your emotional rhythms don't get permanently out of whack. It's about recalibrating your entire emotional system.

This brings us to a paradox that many leaders struggle to accept: You actually become more productive by having a day of rest and building regular seasons of recharging into your life. Over the long haul, you accomplish more by working six focused days than seven depleted ones. It's about effectiveness now and longevity over time. I've always been a hard-charging leader by way of intention. Yet I learned this lesson the tough way when I burned out in 2010. I habitually violated honoring the Sabbath—which has always been Friday for me since I work on the weekends. I realize now that God designed life in such a way that creates increased capacity and sustainability.

When you observe a Sabbath, you're acknowledging that you're not ultimately in control—God is your provider. When you enjoy genuine rest, you're recognizing that your value isn't in what you accomplish but in who you are. This fundamental reorientation is profoundly healing to your emotional life, especially for high-capacity leaders driven by overachievement.

Emotional Recharging Activity:
The Gift of Silence and Solitude

Nineteenth-century Danish philosopher Søren Kierkegaard wrote: "The present state of the world and the whole of life is diseased. If I were a doctor and were asked for my advice, I would reply: Create silence! Bring men to silence. The Word of God cannot be heard in the noisy world of today."[220] And that was 200 years ago!

In our hyperconnected world, perhaps the most countercultural emotional recharging practice is deliberately seeking silence, solitude, and moments of reflection while journaling.

As psychologist Dr. James Pennebaker found, writing about difficult emotional experiences for just fifteen to thirty minutes helps process traumatic events by organizing chaotic thoughts and releasing pent-up emotions.[221] While relationships are vital for building resilience, even the most extroverted leaders need times of intentional withdrawal to process emotions, restore perspective, and refill depleted emotional reserves.

Silence and solitude are essential times of emotional restoration that enable you to be your best for the people you lead. During these quiet periods, your emotional system has space to process experiences that often get buried under the constant demands of leadership.

I find golf by myself to be a powerful emotional recharging activity. Not only does it provide physical exercise, but it creates space for my emotions to settle and my perspective to reset. For you, it might be hiking, fishing, walking, painting, or simply sitting in a favorite chair with no agenda. The specific activity matters less than the intentional separation from the constant stimulation of our world.

Here's a crucial principle: The more intense and pressurized your leadership becomes, the more desperately you need these periods of emotional recharging. Yet, paradoxically, these are the exact times when leaders are most likely to cancel such retreats, considering them optional or indulgent.

Consider building a rhythm of silence and solitude into your leadership schedule. This might look like a monthly half-day, a quarterly full day, or an annual weekend retreat. The format matters less than the consistency and your commitment to create space where your emotional system can recover without constant demands.

During these times, you might include fasting from food, technology, social media, or other activities as an additional practice that sharpens your emotional focus. The withdrawal from these activities serves as a reminder of your deeper hunger for emotional wholeness and renewed perspective in your life and leadership.

Remember, as a leader much of your effectiveness flows from your emotional reserves. Silence and solitude are the hidden foundation that makes your visible leadership truly powerful and sustainable.

Emotional Recharging Activity: Refilling Your Emotional Reserves

Beyond gratitude exercises, Sabbath, and solitude, leaders need regular activities that actively replenish emotional reserves. As Wayne Cordeiro put it: "Do as many of the things that fill your tank as you can. That is how you recharge."[222]

We all have emotional reserves. They form our capacity to handle challenges like disappointment, conflict, grief, or stress without becoming overwhelmed or shutting down. The question is: How full are your emotional reserves? How's your tank?

I remember a time when I was completely emotionally drained. After months of organizational challenges and personal demands, even small decisions felt overwhelming. I recognized I was operating on emotional fumes. So I started intentionally scheduling activities like country drives, walking by the water, and extended times of reading for enjoyment. I knew these would refill my emotional tank. Within weeks, I felt my emotional resilience returning. Decisions that had seemed impossible then felt manageable again.

To help you refuel, take out a piece of paper and make two lists. First, list all the things that fill your emotional tank. These might include traveling, playing sports, spending time in nature, creative pursuits, time with family, and more. Write down anything and everything that recharges you emotionally. Second, list the things that drain your tank. This list may have activities like administrative work, excessive meetings, too much news, endless social media scrolling, being around negative people, or anything else that consistently depletes you.

Now, build a plan to do more of what fills your emotional reserves and less of what drains them. Be especially careful to avoid what I call "counterfeit renewal activities." These are things that might feel like relaxation but actually leave you more depleted. Endless social media scrolling, binge-watching shows, or doomscrolling news sites often masquerade as renewal but actually heighten your adrenaline and deplete your emotional resources.

True emotional recharging activities leave you feeling more energized, more hopeful, and more connected to God, others, and yourself. They don't just distract you from stress; they actively rebuild your capacity to handle it.

The integration of these emotional practices—gratitude walks, Sabbath rest, silence and solitude, and tank-filling activities—creates a comprehensive approach to building emotional resilience. When combined with spiritual connection and mental disciplines, you develop Daniel's "excellent spirit," enabling you to navigate leadership challenges with wisdom, clarity, and steadiness.

How many broken leaders who have derailed their careers and lives would have been well-served by taking more time to refuel? If you're on the edge, it's not too late to stop and recharge!

Fuel for the Mission

As we've explored the three key elements of building inner resilience—spiritual practices, mental disciplines, and emotional habits—we see how powerfully they work together. Daniel's example shows us that resilience isn't just about surviving crises but leading through them with wisdom and purpose. This integration represents the very heart of soul leadership, the foundation upon which all effective, sustainable leadership is built.

Leaders who last practice systematic renewal. They understand that leadership inevitably drains their spiritual, mental, and emotional batteries. Rather than waiting until they're completely depleted, resilient leaders establish regular recharging stations in their lives.

Leaders who last practice systematic renewal.

The integration of these dimensions creates true sustainability in leadership. Your spiritual practices provide the foundation, connecting you to God's perspective and purpose when everything else feels chaotic. Your mental disciplines give you clarity to process challenges with wisdom rather than fear. Your emotional habits allow you to experience authentic feelings without being controlled by them.

This integration doesn't happen automatically. It requires intentional practice before a crisis hits. By establishing rhythms of prayer and Bible engagement, cultivating healthy belief systems, honoring Sabbath rest, creating space for silence and solitude, and filling your emotional reserves, you're building the inner capacity to weather whatever storms come your way.

The resilience equation is now complete. Strong relationships provide your foundation, physical health practices build your structure, and spiritual, mental, and emotional disciplines strengthen your inner core. Together, these create a leadership fortress that can withstand the inevitable pressures and challenges of leading others.

The systematic renewal practices we've discussed aren't separate from your leadership mission. They're essential fuel for it! Soul leadership begins with understanding that your inner world directly impacts your outer influence. The health of your spirit, mind, and emotions inevitably shapes the health of your relationships, decisions, and ultimately, your organization. Remember, healthy leaders heal organizations; hurt leaders hurt organizations. By investing in systematic renewal, you're not just caring for yourself; you're ensuring you have the resources to care for others and fulfill your leadership calling.

Soul leadership begins with understanding that your inner world directly impacts your outer influence.

There's another dimension to explore: the power of integration. In our next chapter, we'll examine the "Shalom Factor"—how the cross of Christ brings healing to the inner fragmentation caused by trauma. The Hebrew concept of *shalom*—wholeness and integrity—offers a compelling vision of what leadership can be when all parts work in harmony. As you continue your journey, remember that God's ultimate goal isn't just to make you resilient; it's to make you whole. It's this wholeness that will ultimately transform not just your leadership but the world you're called to influence.

CHAPTER 9

The Shalom Factor

After Hurricane Katrina hit in 2005, I threw myself into helping our community recover and rebuild. Our church ran drive-through lines for food and essential supplies, cleaned up yards, removed debris, gutted and renovated homes and church buildings, helped people find new employment, assisted with temporary housing, and more. For a whole year I ran on adrenaline, pushing to get our church and community back on their feet. It wasn't until years later that I realized I never had the right tools or understanding to process my own trauma from that event and the following years of helping our region recover.

Looking back, I now see what was missing. I knew how to power through a crisis, but I didn't know how to heal afterward. Ironically, I was trying to help people who'd been traumatized while I myself was a victim of the storm. It took me years to admit I was traumatized in the first place and then learn how to heal. In fact, up to half of all people affected by natural disasters develop some form of significant mental distress or PTSD.[223]

We've talked a lot in this book about how trauma shakes up our lives, fragmenting our brains and disrupting our minds. The intact, integrated brain becomes broken apart—thoughts from feelings, memories from meaning, body from mind. This fragmentation spills over into every part of life: relationships, decision-making, leadership, and even spiritual life.

We've also learned ways to build resilience before crises happen using the resilience equation. With good relationships, taking care of our bodies, and practicing healthy spiritual, mental, and emotional habits, we can increase our resilience to withstand stress and pressure.

But what if you're already hurting? What if you picked up this book not to prepare for future pain but to heal from wounds you're carrying right now? What many of us need is a way to put our broken pieces back together, not just to survive the breaking.

The good news is that healing is possible for you, even years after the crisis has passed. This chapter is for people who are carrying wounds, old or new, just like I was. Since we humans are multifaceted beings, our path to healing is too.

Our *Leaders and Trauma Today* study found that 62 percent of American leaders can feel hopeless when trying to deal with past trauma and extreme adversity.[224] If you're one of them, I'd like to provide some real hope. So let me introduce a post-trauma healing framework I call the shalom factor.

The question at the heart of recovery is this: How do we move from fragmentation to wholeness? How can we experience life as it was intended—integrated, connected, and meaningful? The answer begins with understanding the profound healing power that comes through the cross of Jesus Christ.

The Cross: God's Power to Make Us Whole

In the Old Testament, the prophet Isaiah provided a powerful picture of healing. In Isaiah 53, we read about someone called the "Suffering Servant" who takes on the sin, pain, and suffering of others. In the New Testament, we read that the Suffering Servant was Jesus Christ (Matthew 27:32–56). Isaiah 53:4 says, "Surely He has borne our griefs and carried our sorrows" (NKJV). The word for "carried" is the Hebrew word *sāḇal*, meaning "to bear and carry a burden." The word for "sorrows" is the Hebrew word *makôb*, meaning "mental pain and anguish."[225] Mental pain and anguish are a clear picture of a traumatized person. Therefore, the cross of Christ not only forgives us of our sins but also goes to the core of healing psychological trauma.

The cross of Christ not only forgives us of our sins but also goes to the core of healing psychological trauma.

Jesus also endured punishment to bring peace to those He served (Isaiah 53:4–5). The Hebrew word used here for peace is *shalom*, which, as we introduced in chapter 1, means complete well-being or wholeness. *Shalom* goes far beyond our English understanding of "peace" as just the absence of conflict. It carries the rich meaning of everything being exactly as it should be—body, mind, and spirit—all healthy and working well together. It's about everything being reintegrated, reconnected where we've been disconnected, and restored where we've been damaged. *Shalom* is a state of harmonious existence with God and within ourselves. The atonement of Christ and His sacrifice on the cross allows us to experience peace *with* God—and the peace *of* God—through our faith in Christ and repentance from sin. It is an internal, soul-level peace independent of external circumstances because everything within you is at peace and whole.

The apostle Peter quoted Isaiah saying, "'He himself bore our sins' in his body on the cross [. . .] 'by his wounds you have been healed'" (1 Peter 2:24). This healing—bringing us into a state of *shalom*—is accessible to those who put their faith in Christ.

Yet how does this spiritual reality translate into healing for the traumatized brain and mind? The answer lies in understanding an extraordinary connection between neuroscience and spiritual experience.

The Holy Spirit: Accessing Your Emotional Brain

Psychological trauma is stored in the amygdala within the limbic system, not merely as memories, but as intense emotional imprints. These emotional imprints continue to affect us long after the original danger has passed.[226] This is why traditional "talk therapy" alone often has limited effectiveness for healing trauma. As trauma experts now recognize, just talking about traumatic experiences, what therapists call "top-down" approaches, is insufficient. Top-down therapies primarily focus on the prefrontal cortex (our thought-processing center), which do not fully access the amygdala (our emotional center).[227]

The most effective trauma therapies today focus on what's called a "bottom-up" approach, accessing trauma through the emotional brain first, rather than just through rational thinking. Licensed professional counselor Laurel Boyd, explained it this way:

> Psychologists have realized that if you're just talking about the trauma, you're treating the wrong part of

> the brain. You must access the emotions for processing and healing to happen. A person must feel the feelings associated with various life events, both good and bad.[228]

This is where something remarkable happens in worship and prayer. When you experience the presence of God, whether by worshiping and praying with others or in private, the Holy Spirit does something so powerful researchers are just beginning to understand. He engages your limbic system directly.[229]

Have you ever attended a worship service and found yourself crying while singing and couldn't explain why? Have you witnessed people in prayer experiencing intense emotion, even when they weren't discussing anything sad? What's happening in these moments is profound: The Holy Spirit is engaging those parts of the brain where trauma is stored emotionally. He's bringing healing to memories and wounds you might not even be consciously addressing.

Healing power is found in the peaceful presence of God.

Neuroscience confirms this spiritual reality. As recent research has found, "The ever-expanding concept of neuroplasticity has opened our eyes to the neurophysiological benefits of worship for the brain."[230] Worship that's rooted in God's presence literally shapes us into people who think, feel, and respond more like Christ—what the Bible calls "sanctification." As the apostle Paul said, "May God himself, the God of peace, *sanctify* you through and through. May your whole spirit, soul and body be kept blameless at the coming of our Lord Jesus Christ" (1 Thessalonians 5:23, emphasis added). The research also found that "when we worship, gamma waves are created in our brain that can actually help us feel the presence of God."[231]

What makes this especially powerful for healing trauma is that the Holy Spirit doesn't just work through our rational thought processes. He works through our limbic system—our emotions—the very pathway that trauma experts now recognize as essential for healing.

The indwelling of the Holy Spirit in believers and the presence of God coming upon us during worship—both alone and together with others—literally heals our wounds and reintegrates our brains. This is why we often cry and experience intense joy in worship as the Holy Spirit engages our limbic system. In these moments, we experience *shalom*, or biblical wholeness. Healing power is found in the peaceful presence of God.

The Holy Spirit works to restore and reconnect what sin and trauma have broken apart. This divine activity is truly bottom-up healing, working through our emotions rather than just through our thoughts. We see a powerful example of this kind of complete restoration in how Jesus interacted with those suffering from extreme trauma and mental fragmentation.

The Man of the Tombs

In Mark 5, we see an extreme example of someone who had experienced profound psychological trauma and spiritual bondage. I imagine it looked something like this.

The boat's hull scraped against the shore of the Gerasenes region. As Jesus stepped onto the rocky beach, the disciples still steadying themselves from crossing the Sea of Galilee, an unearthly wail echoed from the cliffs above.

There, silhouetted against the gray sky, stood a man—or what remained of one. His body was a canvas of scars and fresh wounds, blood trickling down his arms where he had slashed himself with sharp stones. His matted hair hung in clumps around a face contorted with anguish. He wore no clothes, his nakedness exposing him to both the elements and the shame few were left to witness. He was so unnaturally strong that no one from the nearby town could restrain him. This was a man in the grip of madness, shattered into countless fragments.

The Holy Spirit works to restore and reconnect what sin and trauma have broken apart.

Jesus addressed the man's fragmented condition with a powerful word of authority (Mark 5:8). The encounter was transformative. The same power and presence that calmed the raging sea now brought peace to this man's tormented mind.

Word spread quickly. People from the nearby town rushed to the scene, expecting to find chaos. Instead, they discovered a profound transformation. There was the man they had once tried to chain, sitting calmly at Jesus's feet. He was dressed in clean clothes. The wild, haunted look had vanished from his eyes—replaced by clarity and peace.

The transformation was complete. The Greek word used to describe him conveys more than just sanity.[232] It says he was "in his right mind" (Mark 5:15). This phrase speaks of wholeness, of a mind brought back into proper balance. The self-harming, isolated, tormented soul had been restored. Where there had been fragmentation, there was now integration. Where there had been severe trauma, there was now *shalom*—complete well-being in body, mind, and spirit.

This is what genuine healing looks like through the power of Christ. Not just relief from symptoms but restoration to community, dignity, and purpose. This man's transformation stands as a vivid testament to the complete healing Christ offers to all who suffer no matter how deep their wounds or how profound their trauma.

Processing Pain Rather Than Running from It

My own post-Katrina journey taught me a lesson: Leaders often bypass the healing provision found at the cross of Christ. We often substitute the genuine peace of God with neurochemical rewards from achievement and productivity—adrenaline and dopamine hits that feel good temporarily but don't address our inner fragmentation.[233] The momentary high of accomplishment becomes an addictive cycle that can prevent true healing.

This is what genuine healing looks like through the power of Christ: not just relief from symptoms but restoration to community, dignity, and purpose.

In 2010, during my own burnout, I finally recognized this pattern. Ultimate recovery happens in the presence of God. Therefore, leaders should not rush past the cross and its provision. Slow down. Worship God. Spend time in His presence and let the Holy Spirit heal your emotions and restore your fragmented mind.

In fact, after going through trauma, leaders in our study believe the best lesson they've learned is to slow down and take care of themselves.[234] This advice runs counter to some leadership strategy that equates effectiveness with constant activity. Yet the most vital healing power is found in God's internal work in our brains, minds, and hearts, which we experience best when we slow down during regular times of reflection.

Perhaps most profoundly, this impacts more than ourselves. Whole leaders create whole organizations. The healing that begins in your own mind and spirit eventually extends to those you lead and serve.

As we've established throughout this book, we weren't meant to walk this path alone. While healing begins with God's presence, it continues through the healing power of community.

Healing Through Authentic, Safe Relationships

While there is healing power in the presence of God, there's another crucial dimension to trauma recovery. Let's revisit relationships. While relationships described in chapter 7 provide a support system for building resilience to mitigate the impact of trauma, relationships are also crucial for post-trauma recovery. The apostle James captured this beautifully when he wrote: "Confess your sins to each other and pray for each other so that you may be healed" (James 5:16 NLT). The Greek word for "healed" here speaks of wholeness—complete restoration.[235] This reveals something profound: We experience healing when we share our wounds and hurts with safe people who pray for us.

This passage isn't just about confessing sin; remaining calm, it's also about sharing our pain, our traumatic experiences, and our hurts with people we trust. When we do this in the context of caring relationships, something remarkable happens: The Holy Spirit works through those connections to access the same emotional regions of our brain where trauma is stored. Just as in worship, this creates a "bottom-up" healing pathway, working through our emotions rather than just through our thoughts.

The principle is sharing something that has wounded you with another and then having them engage by listening, remaining calm, empathizing, and praying for you. It's also what psychologists call "coregulation," the process by which others provide external support as you navigate your emotional experiences.[236] This is why when people talk about painful experiences in a supportive community, they often experience emotional release and healing—even when they couldn't process those emotions alone. When we talk about our trauma with people we trust and receive empathy and healing prayer, our emotional and thinking parts of the brain start to work harmoniously again. This aids in restructuring our brains and helps the broken pieces become whole.[237]

Strong relationships have a profound psychological effect. Researchers studied students at the University of Virginia, taking them to the base of a steep hill and fitting them with a weighted backpack. They were then asked to estimate the hill's steepness. Some participants stood next to friends during the exercise, while others were alone. The students who stood with friends gave lower estimates. The longer the friends had known each other, the less steep the hill appeared.[238]

One of the authors of the study even said, "What we are finding is that things that we have always thought of as having metaphorical value, like friendship, actually affect our physiology. Social support changes how we perceive the world and how our bodies work."[239] Solomon got it right when he wrote, "Two are better than one, because they have a good reward for their labor. For if they fall, one will lift up his companion. But woe to him who is alone when he falls, for he has no one to help him up" (Ecclesiastes 4:9–10 NKJV).

The friends who help us see hills as less steep are valuable. When recovering from trauma, our need for community becomes even greater. The people who help us heal after trauma help us work through our pain in a different way than superficial relationships. As van der Kolk said, "Traumatized human beings recover in the context of relationships."[240]

Yet the nature of leadership itself can lead to an unhealthy self-reliance and lack of community. We need people around us who are trustworthy, available, life-giving, and safe. Remember King Saul? Originally, he had a relationship with Samuel, but the relationship disintegrated. David, by contrast, had close relationships with both Jonathan and Nathan the prophet, and he embraced their input even when it was difficult to hear. That's one reason David recovered from his failures while Saul spiraled downward. These biblical examples illustrate a primary way experts tell us to treat trauma: through healthy processing in safe relationships.[241]

Leaders who have experienced trauma often retreat into isolation precisely when they need connection most. This isolation isn't merely a social choice; it's a neurobiological response. Trauma can cause your brain to view relationships as potential threats rather than sources of healing.[242]

This creates a challenging paradox: The very connections needed for healing become what traumatized leaders avoid.

Trusted relationships create relational safety. In turn, safety can even help increase the size of parts of the brain that are key for trauma recovery.[243] As van der Kolk also noted, "Safety and terror are incompatible. When we are terrified, nothing calms us down like the reassuring voice or the firm embrace of someone we trust."[244]

Proverbs 18:1 also highlights the danger of isolation: "A man who isolates himself seeks his own desire; He rages against all wise judgment" (NKJV). This perfectly describes leaders trapped in isolation. When you see a leader making inexplicable choices that damage their family, ministry, or organization, you're often witnessing an individual with a traumatized brain. Their amygdala is overwhelming their prefrontal cortex. Said differently, their emotions are hijacking their rational thought, leaving them vulnerable to destructive impulses.

During my recovery from trauma in 2010 and beyond, I relied heavily on my close community. These weren't just casual friendships. They were deep, safe relationships where I could process my traumatic experiences without judgment or risk of retraumatization. They created space where I could be completely transparent about my struggles. This connection was crucial to my recovery.

Integration Through Professional Support

While the cross and the *shalom* of God provide spiritual and emotional healing and community offers relational support, sometimes professional counseling is a necessary component in post-trauma recovery. Trauma-informed counseling specifically addresses psychological trauma and helps heal the brain.

Over the years, I've been fortunate to work with a number of trauma-informed therapists who helped me greatly. During a particularly difficult season after my burnout, I worked with a counselor for about a year. He helped me identify unhealthy patterns and misbeliefs that I had brought from my past into the contemporary challenges I experienced in the aftermath of Katrina and the financial crisis of 2008–2010.

It's important to note that many leaders, through Christ's power and healthy relationships, may recover without counseling. Yet, professional help becomes particularly valuable in three scenarios:

1. When trauma symptoms persist despite spiritual practices and community support
2. When the trauma is severe or prolonged and is evidencing PTSD-like criteria (mentioned in chapter 2)
3. When leadership responsibilities demand accelerated recovery

One of the key roles a counselor plays is guiding you through the grieving process; something that's essential for healing but often difficult to navigate alone. Our study found that the death and sickness of a loved one were the most prevalent traumatic events leaders typically face, yet grieving these losses properly is an area of struggle for many.[245] A licensed professional can help you process these losses in a healthy, safe, and therapeutic setting.

Professional counseling for trauma differs from general therapy in its specialized focus on brain reintegration and bottom-up approaches. Below are some of the more common evidence-based modalities that mental health professionals employ to help individuals recovering from trauma. I am not endorsing or recommending any particular treatment. Any treatment plan you undertake should be done so under the consultation of your mental health professional.

- **Experiential Therapy:** Helps people work through painful emotions using techniques such as roleplaying and other therapeutic strategies to promote processing and healing[246]
- **Eye Movement Desensitization and Reprocessing (EMDR):** Uses bilateral stimulation to help the brain process traumatic memories[247]
- **Somatic Therapy:** Addresses how trauma is stored in the body, not just the mind[248]
- **Narrative Therapy:** Helps people reauthor their trauma story from one of victimhood to one of overcoming[249]
- **Brainspotting:** Therapists identify specific eye positions that activate emotional and physical reactions, allowing for deeper processing and healing[250]

Professional counseling offers specialized tools for people navigating the aftermath of trauma, helping restore neural pathways and emotional regulation. When selected thoughtfully, a trauma-informed counselor becomes a valuable guide through the difficult terrain of psychological healing.

Your Journey to *Shalom*

The shalom factor offers a restorative pathway after you have experienced trauma. This three-part approach—the cross, community, and counseling—provides a comprehensive framework for restoring wholeness to leaders who carry trauma's wounds.

The integration of these three elements creates something powerful. The impact of the cross brings together spiritual, emotional, and psychological healing. Neural pathways disrupted by trauma begin to reconnect. The emotional and rational parts of your brain resume healthy communication. You regain the ability to respond thoughtfully rather than react emotionally.

This restoration isn't just personal; it transforms your leadership. When your brain regains integration, your life and leadership begin reflecting that same wholeness. Your clarity of thought improves decision-making. Your emotional regulation enhances relationship-building. And being spiritually grounded provides wisdom in complex situations.

My own journey after Hurricane Katrina and subsequent challenges taught me that trauma recovery doesn't follow a linear path. There were setbacks amid the progress, moments when old trauma responses reasserted themselves even as new, healthier patterns were forming. The key was persistence in all three healing dimensions: continuing to pursue God's presence, remaining connected to my support structure, and doing the hard work of counseling when necessary.

Today, I can testify that post-trauma healing is not only possible but can ultimately deepen your leadership capacity. The very wounds that once threatened to end your leadership can become the foundation for deeper wisdom, greater empathy, and more authentic influence. Your greatest leadership impact still lies ahead. Your trauma can make you a more effective leader who truly understands pain and can help others find healing.

In the next chapter, we'll explore how this newfound integration creates the foundation for post-traumatic growth—turning past pain into future purpose through the growth model.

CHAPTER 10

Growing Forward

When my daughter Isabelle was in college, she was driving when her car was rear-ended in a serious accident. The impact was severe and left a large gash on her head. Then, just six weeks later, when driving with my wife, she was t-boned by a large truck. That second collision caused a severe break to Isabelle's arm, leaving her with a painful injury and a permanent scar.

The orthopedist explained something fascinating during her recovery: When a bone heals from a break, the healing site becomes temporarily stronger than the original bone due to increased calcium deposits during the repair process. The fracture signals the body to send extra resources to the injured area, creating a reinforced point where the break occurred.

This physical healing process mirrors what can happen psychologically after trauma but with a significant difference. While a healed bone eventually returns to its normal strength, psychological healing can create permanent positive changes. Psychological recovery isn't just about returning to baseline; it's about emerging stronger.

Our brains have remarkable flexibility to change and adapt. When we properly process trauma, we not only heal the damage but also develop new mental strengths that make us more resilient, insightful, and compassionate than before.

This phenomenon isn't just anecdotal; it's a well-documented reality for many leaders. In our *Leaders and Trauma Today* study, 79 percent of American leaders said they've been successful in using their difficult experiences to develop deeper wisdom and compassion for people.[251] This remarkable statistic reveals a crucial truth: Crisis, while profoundly challenging, can become a powerful catalyst for your growth.

Crisis, while profoundly challenging, can become a powerful catalyst for your growth.

The good news is that the pressure points of trauma don't just create deficits; they can also reshape us in positive ways when properly processed. This illustrates what research defines as "post-traumatic growth" (PTG), the ability to emerge stronger and better following significant trauma or severe adversity.[252] Resilience is about bouncing back to one's original state after difficulties. PTG, on the other hand, is about leaping forward—advancing beyond the baseline of previous functioning.[253] Leaders who experience PTG find themselves becoming better spouses, parents, mentors, professionals, and more.

Yet PTG does not come easily. It follows intense emotional, psychological, and even spiritual struggle.[254] Leaders who process trauma deliberately and effectively, with the right tools and supportive relationships, are able to harness their hardships as opportunities for profound personal and professional growth.

Understanding Trauma and Growth

Abraham Lincoln's path to becoming one of America's most revered presidents was paved with extraordinary adversity. Before reaching the White House, Lincoln endured a series of crushing setbacks: business failures that left him in debt for over a decade, electoral defeats spanning multiple offices, and profound personal losses including the death of his fiancée Ann Rutledge, which triggered a depression so severe his friends removed weapons from his home.[255] These experiences, rather than defeating him, forged his resilience and deepened his character.

Resilience is about bouncing back to one's original state after difficulties. PTG, on the other hand, is about leaping forward—advancing beyond the baseline of previous functioning.

Through these trials, Lincoln developed the qualities that would define his legendary leadership. His familiarity with failure cultivated a remarkable persistence, while his encounters with grief enhanced his capacity for empathy. This hard-earned wisdom served him and the nation when, as president, he confronted both personal tragedy—the death of his son Willie—and national crisis during the Civil War. Lincoln's journey exemplifies how adversity and trauma can transform into post-traumatic growth, equipping leaders with deeper reservoirs of strength, wisdom, and compassion, which were precisely the qualities needed to guide the nation through difficult times.

Trauma is often perceived purely as negative, a damaging experience that harms our well-being and potential. However, emerging research illustrates a far richer and more hopeful narrative. While our brains possess the incredible capacity of neuroplasticity—rewiring themselves in response to experiences—our mental and emotional selves are also being reshaped through thoughtfully processing difficult circumstances.[256]

Resilience helps prevent the worst effects of trauma, while PTG represents the possibility of benefiting from the struggle with trauma.

The pressure points of trauma can reshape our inner landscape in ways that actually enhance certain capacities. Resilience is central to this process and has been extensively studied, notably among military veterans who faced extreme conditions during the Vietnam War.[257] It's important to note the prevalence of mental health problems among Vietnam veterans led to the official recognition of PTSD as a diagnosis in 1980 by the American Psychological Association.[258] However, some veterans, despite enduring severe adversity, displayed remarkably low rates of long-term psychological problems. Researchers identified key growth traits in these individuals, including:

- Strong social connections and relationships[259]
- Flexible and adaptive thinking[260]
- Clear, deeply held personal values
- Acts of helping others, even under difficult circumstances
- Humor and the ability to maintain perspective

- Constructive methods of facing fears and challenges[261]

The relationship between resilience and post-traumatic growth is both complex and complementary. While they're often discussed together, they represent different aspects of how we respond to crises. Resilience is our ability to maintain functioning and "bounce back" despite difficult circumstances. It helps us withstand the impact of trauma. PTG, on the other hand, is about transformative positive changes that occur specifically because of our struggle with highly challenging circumstances.

Think of it this way: Resilience helps prevent the worst effects of trauma, while PTG represents the possibility of benefiting from the struggle with trauma. Both are valuable, but they operate differently. A highly resilient person might recover quickly from adversity without experiencing significant growth, while someone with less initial resilience might struggle more but ultimately experience profound transformation and enhanced resilience through that struggle.

The most effective approach is to develop both capacities—building resilience to mitigate trauma's immediate impact while remaining open to the growth opportunities that can emerge from properly processing traumatic experiences. For leaders, this dual approach creates a powerful foundation for navigating the inevitable challenges of leadership while continuously evolving into more effective, compassionate guides for those they serve.

The key to unlocking PTG lies in intentional processing, which typically involves seeking professional guidance, leaning heavily on trusted relationships, engaging in meaningful reflection, and often incorporating spiritual practices.[262]

True growth may require stepping back temporarily from leadership responsibilities to prioritize healing, which is exactly what I had to do in 2010. As I came to learn, recognizing this necessity is itself a sign of wisdom and strength. In fact, 69 percent of leaders in our study acknowledge that traumatic experiences taught them to step back momentarily to focus on recovery, setting the stage for deeper, more sustainable growth.[263]

By understanding the interplay between trauma, resilience, and PTG, we can view our most challenging experiences not as insurmountable setbacks but as transformative opportunities. Remember, trauma changes us. The question isn't whether you'll change—but how? Will you choose to grow forward?

Transforming Trauma into Healthy Leadership

Recall King Saul's tragic leadership journey. It shows how unprocessed trauma can lead to downfall through cycles of shame, fear, and control. Saul never successfully integrated his trauma into his leadership; instead, he allowed it to consume him, ultimately destroying his legacy. In contrast, David—despite his own significant traumas—processed his pain through honest lament, authentic relationships, and spiritual connection with both God and others, becoming Israel's greatest king.

Successfully navigating trauma involves more than enduring difficult experiences. It requires thoughtful and intentional incorporation of those experiences into your identity and leadership style. This integration transforms painful memories and hardships into powerful sources of personal strength, authenticity, and compassion.

The start of healthy integration is recognizing the balance required between leadership responsibilities and the essential time needed for personal recovery. Leaders often feel compelled to power through their trauma, mistakenly believing that pausing equates to failure or weakness. However, research shows that leaders who acknowledge their need for recovery and deliberately reorganize their lives to heal emerge stronger and more effective.[264]

> **By understanding the interplay between trauma, resilience, and PTG, we can view our most challenging experiences not as insurmountable setbacks but as transformative opportunities.**

First, taking a step back allows deeper wisdom and compassion. Leaders who experience post-traumatic growth often report heightened sensitivity and greater emotional intelligence. Trauma, when processed well, can significantly enhance our empathy and ability to recognize and respond to the emotional needs of others, creating stronger bonds within teams and organizations.[265]

Second, taking time to reflect helps us strengthen relationships through vulnerability—not an easy task in any situation. Sharing your experiences openly and honestly can foster deeper connections with others. Vulnerability can be mistakenly perceived as a weakness in leadership. However, it actually creates a safe environment, encouraging others to speak openly about their challenges, thus building resilience and cohesion at an organizational level.[266]

Third, we can transform past wounds into strengths. Rather than allowing trauma to harm your sense of self-worth, incorporating these painful experiences helps leaders recognize their inherent strengths and create new capabilities. Leaders often discover newfound clarity, resolve, and a deeper sense of purpose in their roles after effectively processing trauma.

Here are some principles that will help leaders to incorporate processed trauma into healthy leadership:

- Prioritizing personal recovery and emotional well-being, recognizing when to courageously take intentional pauses from leadership demands.
- Actively cultivate empathy by engaging in activities like reflective writing and safe, open conversations in supportive relationships.
- Fostering environments of psychological safety where team members feel encouraged to discuss challenges and seek support openly.

Leaders who integrate their traumatic experiences appropriately are better equipped to create supportive environments for their teams and organizations. Their example provides a powerful model, inspiring others within their organizations to pursue similar growth-oriented journeys. This effort can lead to healthier, more resilient organizations overall.

The goal is not just to get past trauma but to incorporate it into who you become—a wiser, more compassionate, and more effective leader. This is the heart of soul leadership: not denying the wounds but transforming them into wisdom that serves others well.[267]

The Pattern of Post-Traumatic Growth

Remember the biblical character Daniel and his journey. His story illustrates a pattern of post-traumatic growth. He faced the trauma of being forcibly taken from his home. Not once, but twice! Yet through consistent spiritual practices, mental disciplines, and emotional awareness, he emerged stronger.

Understanding PTG involves recognizing the common patterns or stages that we experience as we move from trauma toward transformation. While each person's journey is unique, research highlights several distinct and predictable phases in this journey known as the THRIVE Model, developed by psychologist Stephen Joseph.[268]

T: Taking Stock

The THRIVE Model begins with taking stock of the situation following trauma. In this initial phase, leaders must first ensure their physical and emotional safety. Practical measures such as adequate rest, medical care, and secure surroundings create a foundation for recovery. It's also essential at this stage to acknowledge and accept one's emotional reactions like anger, fear, confusion, or grief without judgment or suppression.

When Hurricane Katrina devastated New Orleans, my first response had to be practical—ensuring my family's safety, helping our church members find shelter, and addressing immediate physical needs. Only after these basic needs were met could I begin to process the emotional impact of what had happened. The same will be true for you.

H: Harvesting Hope

Hope is a critical catalyst for growth after trauma. Leaders often find hope through inspirational examples of others who have successfully navigated trauma. Engaging with stories of resilience and growth can reignite optimism and inspire perseverance. Leaning into social support networks and trusted relationships also nurtures hope, providing both emotional encouragement and practical advice.

During my recovery period in 2010–2012, reading the stories of other leaders who had experienced burnout and trauma, such as Peter Scazzero, Wayne Cordeiro, and others, only to return stronger, gave me hope that my own leadership journey wasn't over.

When we rewrite our trauma stories from a perspective of growth rather than victimhood, we actually begin to rewire our brains, creating new neural pathways that support healing and resilience.

R: Re-Authoring

A powerful component of PTG involves reframing traumatic experiences through a growth mindset. Leaders who intentionally reinterpret their stories by focusing on what they've learned and how they've positively changed create a compelling narrative for themselves and others. This stage often involves expressive practices, such as journaling or storytelling, which research has shown to significantly enhance psychological well-being.[269]

When we rewrite our trauma stories from a perspective of growth rather than victimhood, we actually begin to rewire our brains, creating new neural pathways that support healing and resilience.[270] This renewing of the mind transforms not only how we think about our experiences but how our brain physically processes them.

I: Identifying Change

As leaders progress through their trauma recovery, noticing and acknowledging positive changes is critical. Documenting shifts in personal strength, deeper relationships, greater empathy, or new perspectives on life reinforces these gains. This recognition serves as motivation to continue the hard work of transformation.

After my recovery, I noticed that I had developed greater empathy for others who were struggling. I was less judgmental of leaders who hit walls of exhaustion, and I became more intentional about creating sustainable rhythms in my own life and leadership. Acknowledging these positive changes helped me see value in what had been an incredibly painful experience.

V: Valuing the Change

Gratitude also plays an integral role in post-traumatic growth. This doesn't mean you must be grateful for the traumatic event that happened to you; but rather, you can be thankful for the help and resources surrounding you in the midst of your pain. Leaders who regularly practice gratitude by appreciating the positive changes they've experienced—even while acknowledging their ongoing struggles—report enhanced emotional resilience and greater overall life satisfaction.[271] As Scripture encourages us: "Consider it pure joy, my brothers and sisters, whenever you face trials of many kinds, because you know that the testing of your faith produces perseverance. Let perseverance finish its work so that you may be mature and complete, not lacking anything" (James 1:2–4).

Spiritual disciplines like prayer, Scripture engagement, worship, and Sabbath-keeping create space for gratitude to take root, helping us recognize God's presence and provision even in our most difficult seasons. This practice of thanksgiving shifts our focus from what we've lost to what we've gained.

E: Expressing Change in Action

Translating internal growth into tangible actions solidifies PTG. Leaders often discover meaningful ways to help others facing similar struggles, transforming their experiences into opportunities for mentorship, advocacy, or organizational change. Helping others not only reinforces personal growth but also fosters a stronger sense of purpose and community. A great example of this kind of mentorship is seen among those who have found recovery through Alcoholics Anonymous. Those who have gained sobriety, and now give back as sponsors, demonstrate how expressing change through service strengthens personal growth.

What began as personal pain can become a resource for others. Consider the interrelated stories of John Walsh and Elizabeth Smart.[272] Walsh experienced unimaginable pain when his six-year-old son, Adam, was abducted and tragically murdered in 1981. Determined to redeem his grief, Walsh channeled his suffering into activism, eventually launching the groundbreaking television show *America's Most Wanted*. The show leveraged collective empathy and public vigilance to solve crimes and rescue victims.

Elizabeth Smart was abducted from her Utah home in 2002, sparking a nationwide search. Her story aired prominently on *America's Most Wanted*, mobilizing countless viewers. As a direct result of Walsh's tireless efforts, born from his personal tragedy, Elizabeth Smart was recognized and rescued after nine harrowing months in captivity. John Walsh is a great example of putting change into action.

I've seen this pattern repeated in many leaders who've navigated trauma and emerged with something valuable to offer. I've found that my own experiences with trauma and recovery have given me a platform to help other leaders recognize warning signs and develop healthier practices.

By clearly understanding and embracing the THRIVE Model, leaders can actively guide their recovery, moving intentionally from trauma toward transformation. This structured yet flexible framework provides a powerful roadmap for those who wish to transform their hardships into enduring strengths both personally and professionally.

Our darkest moments often contain the seeds of our greatest growth.

What the Bible Says About Growing Forward

Modern research on trauma and PTG aligns closely with powerful insights offered in Scripture. The Bible explicitly acknowledges suffering and adversity as inevitable parts of our human experiences. Yet, it emphasizes that these challenges hold transformative potential when approached with faith and perseverance.

Consider Joseph's story from the Old Testament book of Genesis. Joseph was betrayed by his brothers, sold into slavery, falsely accused, and imprisoned because of it. He endured traumas that would have broken most people. Yet those ordeals refined Joseph's character rather than destroying it.

His suffering cultivated wisdom, patience, and remarkable forgiveness. When finally reunited with the very brothers who had sold him, Joseph demonstrated a profound perspective. He said, "You intended to harm me, but God intended it all for good. He brought me to this position so I could save the lives of many people" (Genesis 50:20 NLT). Faith can transform suffering into strength and purpose. Our darkest moments often contain the seeds of our greatest growth.

It's important to remember trauma can originate from various sources: some of them being our own choices, the choices of others, or circumstances beyond our control. Regardless of your situation, the biblical principles for growth remain consistent. The source of your trauma doesn't disqualify you from growth; it simply shapes your journey toward it.

Comfort From God

In moments of suffering, the comfort leaders receive from their faith can be transformative. Scripture highlights how this divine comfort isn't merely meant to soothe the individual but also equips them to comfort others facing similar struggles (2 Corinthians 1:3–4). By embracing this perspective, leaders can transform their own comfort into empathy and support for others.

This biblical principle directly supports the pattern of post-traumatic growth. The comfort we receive becomes a resource we can offer to others, creating a beautiful cycle of healing that extends far beyond our personal experience. This is *shalom* in action: wholeness that spreads from one life to another.

Building Character

Suffering, when faced with endurance and faith, produces perseverance, character, and ultimately hope (Romans 5:3–5). This progression reflects the core stages identified by modern research into PTG. Leaders can rely on this biblical insight to frame their crises as formative experiences rather than destructive setbacks.

Our responses to suffering actually shape who we become. When we persevere through trials with faith, we develop qualities that wouldn't—*perhaps couldn't*—emerge any other way. The brain's neuroplasticity mirrors this spiritual truth: We are literally being transformed through our responses to life's challenges.

Hope-Filled Perspective

As Romans 8:28 says, "And we know that all things work together for good to those who love God, to those who are the called according to His purpose" (NKJV). This verse reminds leaders that current hardships, no matter how intense, have a God-redeeming purpose. This hope-filled perspective helps leaders maintain resilience and patience during prolonged difficulties. This is powerfully illustrated in the life of NFL quarterback Drew Brees, whose personal comeback story became intertwined with an entire city's renewal.

When Brees arrived in New Orleans, his career was hanging by a thread.[273] After suffering a devastating shoulder injury while playing for San Diego, the Chargers released him, uncertain he'd ever fully recover. Yet, as Brees would later say, "God, I know that if you bring me to it, you will bring me through it."[274] With unwavering faith and determination, he turned his adversity into an opportunity, choosing optimism over self-pity: "I realized I could focus on my mistakes and feel sorry for myself, or I could learn from those mistakes and use them as motivation to come back stronger."[275]

What makes Brees's story particularly powerful is the timing. He joined the Saints in 2006, just months after Hurricane Katrina had devastated New Orleans. The broken quarterback found himself in a broken city—and both would heal together. Brees even wrote in his memoir *Coming Back Stronger* that "we couldn't ignore the irresistible feeling—a sense of spiritual calling, even—that God wanted us in New Orleans."[276]

Brees didn't just rehabilitate his shoulder; he became a beacon of hope and resilience for a community desperate for healing. The adversity he faced transformed him into a more compassionate leader, enabling him to inspire others enduring their own struggles. Through faith and perseverance, Brees didn't merely return to football. He led the Saints to their first-ever Super Bowl victory in 2010, while also establishing a foundation that has contributed over $45 million to improve the quality of life for people in need.

Drew Brees's story illustrates the biblical principle that our deepest wounds, when properly processed, can become our greatest platform for impact. As God said to the apostle Paul, "My grace is sufficient for you, for my power is made perfect in weakness" (2 Corinthians 12:9).

God's Purpose

As Holocaust survivor Viktor Frankl observed in his landmark work *Man's Search for Meaning*, "In some ways suffering ceases to be suffering at the moment it finds a meaning."[277] For leaders, connecting our suffering to a bigger purpose of helping others provides exactly this kind of redemptive meaning.

This perspective doesn't minimize suffering or suggest that traumatic experiences should somehow be pursued. Rather, it acknowledges the reality of pain while offering a framework for finding meaning and growth within it.

Scripture assures us that even our most challenging experiences are never wasted. As 1 Peter 5:10 says, "And after you have suffered a little while, the God of all grace, who has called you to his eternal glory in Christ, will himself restore, confirm, strengthen, and establish you" (ESV). This passage perfectly aligns with the reality of post-traumatic growth. What science is now discovering, Scripture has been teaching for millennia: Pain, when properly processed, can become purposeful.

Pain, when properly processed, can become purposeful.

Transforming Leadership and Organizations

When a leader heals, the effects extend far beyond their personal well-being. They lift the lid on what's possible for everyone around them. Emotionally healthy, spiritually grounded, and psychologically resilient leaders create cultures where people can thrive. These cultures are marked by psychological safety, open communication, and shared strength.

A fragmented leader creates fragmented organizations, while a whole leader fosters integration throughout their team and culture. This is why soul leadership is so crucial! The wholeness or fragmentation within a leader inevitably reproduces itself in the systems and relationships they influence.

Leaders who overcome hardship often discover a deeper sense of purpose. They typically become more committed to creating environments where others can grow. These leaders become what we might call "healing agents" in their organizations. They model vulnerability, prioritize well-being, and invest in people, not just performance.

Organizational transformation doesn't happen by accident. It requires intentional design and consistent practice. Leaders who have walked through trauma and emerged stronger can implement systems and habits that reflect the values they've developed.

The journey of post-traumatic growth is not a quick fix. It takes time, intentionality, and ongoing effort. But for those who commit to it, the results are profound.

The Soul Leadership Cycle

Author Sam Chand said, "If you're not hurting, you're not leading."[278] This is why soul leadership is necessary. Leadership pain is inevitable. A true leader cannot move an organization forward without caring deeply for the people they lead. When you care for people, you share in their hurts and pains. Your successful navigation of crisis into post-traumatic growth and wholeness will help you guide others in health and effectiveness in their own life and leadership.

This cycle isn't just a conceptual framework; it's a practical roadmap for leaders navigating the inevitable challenges of life and leadership. First, we recognize how trauma and triggers affect us. Then, we build resilience through key relationships, physical health, and spiritual, mental, and emotional disciplines. Finally, we embrace the growth model that allows us to emerge stronger, wiser, and more compassionate.

The journey from trauma to transformation isn't easy, but it is definitely possible when guided by soul leadership. The destination of resilience, wholeness, and growth is worth every step.

As you continue your own leadership journey, remember that your wounds don't disqualify you. In fact, when properly processed, they become your greatest sources of wisdom, compassion, and impact.

I recently spoke at a conference to thousands of leaders sharing the principles of soul leadership. Afterward I took time to listen to many who had also suffered traumatic experiences in their lives and leadership. I was humbled and even brought to tears as I heard their stories and how my message brought them hope. I realized it was all worth it. On the day I crashed, I delivered a sermon with shaking and trembling hands. But at this conference, I stood with quiet confidence and reassurance that my experience had redemptive power. In 2010, I didn't imagine that fifteen years later my pain would be filled with so much purpose by helping others.

When you lead from a place of wholeness rather than fragmentation, you create space for others to do the same. This is the essence of soul leadership. My prayer is that this book will bring you hope and healing on your journey toward *shalom*.

Acknowledgments

To Dr. Tom Mullins, my coach, role model, and doctoral mentor—

Thank you for modeling what it means to lead with strength, humility, and integrity. Your wisdom, support, and steady voice have shaped my life and leadership more than words can express. *Soul Leadership* would not exist today without your encouragement to pursue my doctorate and to write my dissertation on trauma and leaders.

To Dr. Chris Adams, Dr. Scott Adams, Laurel Boyd, Lee Castello, Jim Cress, Dr. Michael Leeman, Dr. Jim Vigil, and Dr. Andy Yarborough—

Each of you played a significant role in helping shape this message—with your scholarly insight, clinical expertise, and commitment to emotional and spiritual health. Thank you for walking with me through this process, for sharpening my thinking, and for standing with me in the vision of helping leaders live and lead from wholeness.

To Pastor Jacob Aranza and Pastor Jim Laffoon—

Thank you for faithfully pastoring Jennifer and me over the past thirty years. Your consistency, intentionality, and wisdom have deeply shaped who I am. Through every season of life, marriage, and ministry, you've stood with us. I could not have written this book without your influence and investment in our lives.

To the amazing team at Church of the King—

Your commitment to leading with integrity, compassion, and spiritual health is transforming lives and advancing God's kingdom around the world. Thank you for living the message of this book!

Notes

1. s.v. “שָׁלוֹם (*shalom*),” in *A Concise Hebrew and Aramaic Lexicon of the Old Testament: Based on the First, Second, and Third Editions of Koehler-Baumgartner,* ed. William L. Holladay (Grand Rapids, MI: Eerdmans, 1971).
2. Allison Plyer, “Facts for Features: Katrina Impact,” The Data Center, August 26, 2016, accessed July 8, 2025, https://www.datacenterresearch.org/data-resources/katrina/facts-for-impact/.
3. Robert Kayen et al., “USGS Scientists Investigate New Orleans Levees Broken by Katrina,” Sound Waves 2006, no. 79 (December 2005–January 2006), https://archive.usgs.gov/archive/sites/soundwaves.usgs.gov/2006/01/index.html.
4. “2005 Hurricane Katrina: Facts, FAQs, and How to Help,” World Vision, updated November 20, 2023, accessed March 18, 2025, https://www.worldvision.org/disaster-relief-news-stories/2005-hurricane-katrina-facts.
5. Ethan J. Raker et al., “Twelve Years Later: The Long-Term Mental Health Consequences of Hurricane Katrina,” *Social Science and Medicine* 242 (2019): 112610, https://doi.org/10.1016/j.socscimed.2019.112610.
6. Mary Alice Mills et al., “Trauma and Stress Response Among Hurricane Katrina Evacuees,” *American Journal of Public Health* 97, suppl. 1 (2007): S116–23, https://doi.org/10.2105/AJPH.2006.086678.
7. Sandro Galea et al., “Exposure to Hurricane-Related Stressors and Mental Illness After Hurricane Katrina,” *Arch Gen Psychiatry* 64, no. 12 (2007):1427–34, https://doi.org/10.1001/archpsyc.64.12.1427.
8. National Council for Behavioral Health, “How to Manage Trauma,” National Council for Behavioral Health, infographic, August 2022, accessed March 18, 2025, https://www.thenationalcouncil.org/wp-content/uploads/2022/08/Trauma-infographic.pdf.
9. *Leaders and Trauma Today.*
10. Bessel van der Kolk, *The Body Keeps the Score: Brain, Mind, and Body in the Healing of Trauma* (Penguin Books, 2014), 97.
11. APA Dictionary of Psychology, “trauma,” American Psychological Association,

updated April 19, 2018, accessed on November 13, 2019, https://dictionary.apa.org/trauma.

12. K. T. Mueser et al., "Psychometric Evaluation of Trauma and Posttraumatic Stress Disorder Assessments in Persons with Severe Mental Illness," *Psychological Assessment* 13, no. 1 (2001): 110–17, https://doi.org/10.1037/1040-3590.13.1.110.
13. APA Dictionary of Psychology, "crisis," APA, updated April 19, 2018, accessed on November 13, 2019, https://dictionary.apa.org/crisis.
14. Rosana E. Norman et al., "The Long-Term Health Consequences of Child Physical Abuse, Emotional Abuse, and Neglect: A Systematic Review and Meta-Analysis," *PLOS Medicine* 9, no. 11 (2012): e1001349, https://doi.org/10.1371/journal.pmed.1001349.
15. Borja Luque Martinez, "Abandonment Trauma from a Developmental Perspective and Its Treatment," *Seven Editora* (2023), https://doi.org/10.56238/methofocusinterv1-041.
16. Richard A. Bryant et al., "The Psychiatric Sequelae of Traumatic Injury," *American Journal of Psychiatry* 167, no. 3 (2010): 312–20, https://doi.org/10.1176/appi.ajp.2009.09050617.
17. L. Arseneault et al., "Bullying Victimization in Youths and Mental Health Problems: 'Much Ado About Nothing'?," *Psychological Medicine* 40, no. 5 (2010): 717–29, https://doi.org/10.1017/S0033291709991383.
18. Katherine M. Keyes et al., "The Burden of Loss: Unexpected Death of a Loved One and Psychiatric Disorders Across the Life Course in a National Study," *American Journal of Psychiatry* 171, no. 8 (August 2014): 864–71, https://doi:10.1176/appi.ajp.2014.13081132.
19. Joan B. Kelly and Robert Emery, "Children's Adjustment Following Divorce: Risk and Resilience Perspectives," *Family Relations* 52, no. 4 (2003): 352–62, https://doi.org/10.1111/j.1741-3729.2003.00352.x.
20. J. J. Freyd, *Betrayal Trauma: The Logic of Forgetting Childhood Abuse* (Harvard University Press, 1996).
21. K. A. Vickerman and G. Margolin, "Posttraumatic Stress in Children and Adolescents Exposed to Family Violence: II. Treatment," *Professional Psychology: Research and Practice* 38, no. 6 (2007): 620–28, https://doi.org/10.1037/0735-7028.38.6.620.
22. Fran H. Norris et al., "60,000 Disaster Victims Speak: Part I. An Empirical Review of the Empirical Literature, 1981–2001," *Psychiatry: Interpersonal and Biological Processes* 65, no. 3 (2002): 207–39, https://doi.org/10.1521/psyc.65.3.207.20173.
23. Catherine DeCarlo Santiago et al., "Poverty and Mental Health: How Do Low-Income Adults and Children Fare in Psychotherapy?," *Journal of Clinical*

Psychology 69, no. 2 (2013): 115–26, https:doi.org/10.1002/jclp.21951.

24. Mina Fazel et al., "Mental Health of Displaced and Refugee Children Resettled in High-Income Countries: Risk and Protective Factors," *The Lancet* 379, no. 9812 (2012): 266–82, https://doi.org/10.1016/S0140-6736(11)60051-2.
25. Kristin Turney, "Adverse Childhood Experiences Among Children of Incarcerated Parents," *Children and Youth Services Review* 89 (2018): 218–25, https://doi.org/10.1016/j.childyouth.2018.04.033.
26. William Berger et al., "Rescuers at Risk: A Systematic Review and Meta-Regression Analysis of the Worldwide Current Prevalence and Correlates of PTSD in Rescue Workers," *Social Psychiatry and Psychiatric Epidemiology* 47 (2012): 1001–11, https://doi.org/10.1007/s00127-011-0408-2.
27. Ping Guo et al., "Compounded Trauma: A Qualitative Study of the Challenges for Refugees Living with Advanced Cancer," *Palliative Medicine* 35, no. 5 (2021): 916–26, https://doi.org/10.1177/02692163211000236.
28. J. Douglas Bremner, "Traumatic Stress: Effects on the Brain," *Dialogues in Clinical Neuroscience* 8, no. 4 (2006): 445–61, https://doi.org/10.31887/DCNS.2006.8.4/jbremner.
29. Chris Adams et al., "Flourishing in Ministry: A Meta-Model for Clergy Wellbeing Research," *Journal of Psychology and Christianity* 44, no. 1 (2025): 96–107.
30. Pierre Pichère and Anne-Christine Cadiat, *Maslow's Hierarchy of Needs: Gain Vital Insights into How to Motivate People*, trans. Carly Probert (50minutes.com, 2015), 3–4.
31. Wuwei Gong and Susan A. Geertshuis, "Distress and Eustress: An Analysis of the Stress Experiences of Offshore International Students," *Frontiers in Psychology* 14 (2023): 1144767, https://doi.org/10.3389/fpsyg.2023.1144767.
32. Christian T. Elbæk et al., "On the Psychology of Bonuses: The Effects of Loss Aversion and Yerkes-Dodson Law on Performance in Cognitively and Mechanically Demanding Tasks," *Journal of Behavioral and Experimental Economics* 98 (2022): 101870, https://doi.org/10.1016/j.socec.2022.101870.
33. Yale Medicine, "Chronic Stress," accessed March 11, 2025, https://www.yalemedicine.org/conditions/stress-disorder.
34. Razia A. G. Khammissa et al., "Burnout Phenomenon: Neurophysiological Factors, Clinical Features, and Aspects of Management," *Journal of International Medical Research* 50, no. 9 (2022), https://doi.org/10.1177/03000605221106428.
35. Jaryd Hiser et al., "Decision-Making for Concurrent Reward and Threat Is Differentially Modulated by Trauma Exposure and PTSD Symptom Severity," *Behaviour Research and Therapy* 167 (2023): 104361, https://doi.org/10.1016/j.brat.2023.104361.

36. Ryan Gottfredson and William J. Becker, "How Past Trauma Impacts Emotional Intelligence: Examining the Connection," *Frontiers in Psychology* 14 (2023), https://doi.org/10.3389/fpsyg.2023.1067509.
37. Gottfredson and Becker, "How Past Trauma Impacts Emotional Intelligence."
38. David Kinnaman and Nicole Martin, eds., *Trauma in America: Understanding How People Face Hardship and How the Church Offers Hope* (Barna Group, 2020), 29.
39. Felicia Gould et al., "Prior Trauma-Related Experiences Predict the Development of Posttraumatic Stress Disorder After a New Traumatic Event," *Depression and Anxiety* 38, no. 1 (2021): 40–47, https://doi.org/10.1002/da.23084.
40. Patrick R. Steffen et al., "The Brain Is Adaptive Not Triune: How the Brain Responds to Threat, Challenge, and Change," *Frontiers in Psychiatry* 13 (2022): 802606, https://doi.org/10.3389/fpsyt.2022.802606.
41. Cleveland Clinic, "Limbic System," last reviewed April 6, 2024, https://my.clevelandclinic.org/health/body/limbic-system.
42. Björn Rasch and Jan Born, "About Sleep's Role in Memory," *Physiological Reviews* 93, no. 2 (2013): 681–766, https://doi.org/10.1152/physrev.00032.2012.
43. Dominique Debanne et al., "Axon Physiology," *Physiological Reviews* 91, no. 2 (2011): 555–602, https://doi.org/10.1152/physrev.00048.2009.
44. Katie Rapcoch, "Rewiring the Brain After Childhood Trauma: Reclaim Your Life," Re-Origin Technologies, May 10, 2024, updated December 9, 2024, https://www.re-origin.com/articles/rewiring-the-brain-after-childhood-trauma.
45. Xin Zhang et al., "Stress-Induced Functional Alterations in Amygdala: Implications for Neuropsychiatric Diseases, *Frontiers in Neuroscience* 12 (2018): 367, https://doi.org/10.3389/fnins.2018.00367.
46. Steven C. Cramer et al., "Harnessing Neuroplasticity for Clinical Applications," *Brain* 134, no. 6 (2011): 1591–1609, https://doi.org/10.1093/brain/awr039.
47. Jane X. Wang et al., "Covert Rapid Action-Memory Simulation (CRAMS): A Hypothesis of Hippocampal-Prefontal Interactions for Adaptive Behavior," *Neurobiology of Learning and Memory* 117 (2015): 22–33, https://doi.org/10.1016/j.nlm.2014.04.003.
48. Substance Abuse and Mental Health Services Administration, "Child Trauma," updated December 3, 2024, accessed April 16, 2025, https://www.samhsa.gov/mental-health/trauma-violence/child-trauma.
49. Center for Substance Abuse Treatment (US), "Understanding the Impact of Trauma," chap. 3 in *Trauma-Informed Care in Behavioral Health Services*, in *Treatment Improvement Protocol (TIP) Series*, no. 57 (Substance Abuse and Mental Health Services Administration (US), 2014), https://www.ncbi.nlm.

nih.gov/books/NBK207191/.

50. Daniel Cruz et al., "Developmental Trauma: Conceptual Framework, Associated Risks and Comorbidities, and Evaluation and Treatment," *Frontiers in Psychiatry* 13 (2022): 800687, https://doi.org/10.3389/fpsyt.2022.800687.
51. Martin H. Teicher et al., "The Neurobiological Consequences of Early Stress and Childhood Maltreatment," *Neuroscience & Biobehavioral Reviews* 27, nos. 1–2 (2003): 33–44, https://doi.org/10.1016/s0149-7634(03)00007-1.
52. J. L. Herman, "Complex PTSD: A Syndrome in Survivors of Prolonged and Repeated Trauma," *Journal of Traumatic Stress* 5, no. 3 (1992): 377–391, https://doi.org/10.1002/jts.2490050305.
53. Ulrike Zetsche, "The Effects of Rumination on Mood and Intrusive Memories After Exposure to Traumatic Material: An Experimental Study," *Journal of Behavioral Therapy and Experimental Psychiatry* 40, no. 4 (2009): 499–514, https://doi.org/10.1016/j.jbtep.2009.07.001.
54. Mary A. O'Neal et al., "Effects of Fragmentation and the Case for Greater Cohesion in Neurologic Care Delivery," *Neurology* 98, no. 4 (2022): 146–53, https://doi.org/10.1212/WNL.0000000000013079.
55. Sourya Acharya and Samarth Shukla, "Mirror Neurons: Enigma of the Metaphysical Modular Brain," *Journal of Natural Science, Biology and Medicine* 3, no. 2 (2012): 118–24, https://doi.org/10.4103/0976-9668.101878.
56. Cleveland Clinic, "Depersonalization-Derealization Disorder," last modified October 17, 2022, https://my.clevelandclinic.org/health/diseases/9791-depersonalization-derealization-disorder.
57. Alan L. Yuille, "Lecture 16: Hebbian Learning and Regression," lecture slides for Probabilistic Models of the Visual Cortex course, Johns Hopkins University, fall 2020, accessed July 15, 2025, https://www.cs.jhu.edu/~ayuille/JHUcourses/ProbabilisticModelsOfVisualCognition2020/Lec6/HebbianYuilleKersten.pdf.
58. Bart Geurts, "Making Sense of Self Talk," *Review of Philosophy and Psychology* 9 (2018): 271–85, https://doi.org/10.1007/s13164-017-0375-y.
59. Michael Craft, "Finishing Well," *Michael Craft: He > I* (blog), May 19, 2016, https://michaelcraft.org/blog-post/862/.
60. O. S. Hawkins, "Rebuilding: Rebuilders Finish Strong—Part 6," O. S. Hawkins, May 7, 2021, https://www.oshawkins.com/sermons/rebuilders-finish-strong/.
61. Craft, "Finishing Well."
62. Jan Grimell, "Contemporary Insights from Biblical Combat Veterans Through the Lenses of Moral Injury and Post-Traumatic Stress Disorder," *Journal of Pastoral Care and Counseling* 72, no. 4 (2018): 241–50, https://doi.org/10.1177/1542305018790218. Saul as one who suffers from PTSD is well attested in recent scholarly literature. Grimell examined Saul at length as an

example of a biblical character suffering from PTSD; Brad Kelle, *The Bible and Moral Injury* (Abingdon, 2020), 43–67. Kelle laid out a case for Saul as a person suffering from war trauma due to moral injury.

63. Rachel Yehuda and Amy Lehrner, "Intergenerational Transmission of Trauma Effects: Putative Role of Epigenetic Mechanisms," *World Psychiatry: Official Journal of the World Psychiatric Association (WPA)* 17, no. 3 (2018): 243–57, https://doi.org/10.1002/wps.20568.
64. Eric Alan Mitchell, "'Give Us a King': The Triumph of Satire in 1 Samuel 8," PhD diss, The Southern Baptist Theological Seminary, 2023; Moshe Garsiel, The First Book of Samuel: A Literary Study of Comparative Structures, Analogies and Parallels (Jerusalem: Rubin Mass Ltd., 1990). Hebrew version (Ramat-Gan, Israel: Revivim, 1985). Mitchell demonstrates the satirical nature of 1 Samuel 8–10, focusing on chapter eight. Extrapolating from Mitchell's work, one can undertake Garsiel's literary-synchronic method of analysis on chapter nine, noting the sophisticated system of linkages and guidance. The subtle analogies in the book of Samuel suggests Saul was so incompetent that his own father lacked confidence in him.
65. Restoring the Foundations, *Healing and Freedom* (Restoring the Foundations, 2016), 40.
66. Restoring the Foundations, *Healing and Freedom.*
67. Clinton Free et al., "Management Controls: The Organizational Fraud Triangle of Leadership, Culture and Control in Enron," *Ivey Business Journal* (2007), https://iveybusinessjournal.com/publication/management-controls-the-organizational-fraud-triangle-of-leadership-culture-and-control-in-enron/.
68. Karys M. Normansell and Blair E. Wisco, "Negative Interpretation Bias as a Mechanism of the Relationship Between Rejection Sensitivity and Depressive Symptoms" *Cognition and Emotion* 31, no. 5 (2017): 950–62, https://doi.org/10.1080/02699931.2016.1185395.
69. Normansell and Wisco, "Negative Interpretation Bias."
70. Cleveland Clinic, "Rejection Sensitive Dysphoria (RSD): Symptoms & Treatment," last reviewed August 30, 2022, https://my.clevelandclinic.org/health/diseases/24099-rejection-sensitive-dysphoria-rsd.
71. Cleveland Clinic, "Rejection Sensitive Dysphoria (RSD)."
72. *Leaders and Trauma Today.*
73. Peter Cohan, "4 Startling Insights into Elizabeth Holmes from Psychiatrist Who's Known Her Since Childhood," *Forbes*, February 17, 2019, https://www.forbes.com/sites/petercohan/2019/02/17/4-startling-insights-into-elizabeth-holmes-from-psychiatrist-whos-known-here-since-childhood/.
74. Zaw Thiha Tun, "Theranos: A Fallen Unicorn," Investopedia, February 1, 2016, updated March 21, 2025, https://www.investopedia.com/articles/

investing/020116/theranos-fallen-unicorn.asp.

75. *Forbes*, "Elizabeth Holmes," profile, accessed April 16, 2025, https://www.forbes.com/profile/elizabeth-holmes/.
76. Colin McEvoy and Tim Ott, "Inside Elizabeth Holmes and the Downfall of Theranos," *Biography*, last updated May 18, 2023, https://www.biography.com/crime/elizabeth-holmes-theranos-scam.
77. Peter Cohan, "4 Startling Insights into Elizabeth Holmes."
78. Ben Popken and Cyrus Farivar, "Elizabeth Holmes Testifies College Rape, Partner's Control Fueled Drive," NBC News, November 29, 2021, https://www.nbcnews.com/business/business-news/elizabeth-holmes-testifies-college-rape-partners-control-fueled-drive-rcna6925.
79. Bobby Allyn, "Elizabeth Holmes Testifies About Alleged Sexual and Emotional Abuse at Fraud Trial," NPR, November 29, 2021, https://www.npr.org/2021/11/29/1059916883/elizabeth-holmes-testimony-trial-theranos.
80. Popken and Farivar, "Elizabeth Holmes Testifies College Rape."
81. *Leaders and Trauma Today.*
82. Center for Substance Abuse Treatment (US), "Understanding the Impact of Trauma," chap. 3 in *Trauma-Informed Care in Behavioral Health Services*, in *Treatment Improvement Protocol (TIP) Series*, no. 57 (Substance Abuse and Mental Health Services Administration (US), 2014), https://www.ncbi.nlm.nih.gov/books/NBK207191/; Ismar Alburquerque, "Unresolved Trauma: Signs, Causes, & Treatment," Choosing Therapy, October 23, 2024, https://www.choosingtherapy.com/unresolved-trauma/; National Child Traumatic Stress Network, "Effects," accessed May 11, 2025, https://www.nctsn.org/what-is-child-trauma/trauma-types/complex-trauma/effects; Center for Substance Abuse Treatment (US), "Understanding the Impact of Trauma," chap. 3 in *Trauma-Informed Care in Behavioral Health Services*, in *Treatment Improvement Protocol (TIP) Series*, no. 57 (Substance Abuse and Mental Health Services Administration (US), 2014), https://www.ncbi.nlm.nih.gov/books/NBK207191/.
83. Giancarlo Dimaggio et al., "The Problem of Overcontrol: Perfectionism, Emotional Inhibition, and Personality Disorders," *Comprehensive Psychiatry* 83 (2018): 71–78, https://doi.org/10.1016/j.comppsych.2018.03.005.
84. *Leaders and Trauma Today.*
85. Wayne Cordeiro, *Leading on Empty: Refilling Your Tank and Renewing Your Passion* (Baker Publishing Group, 2010).
86. Judith A. Okely et al., "The Interaction Between Stress and Positive Affect in Predicting Mortality," *Journal of Psychosomatic Research* 100 (2017): 53–60, https://doi.org/10.1016/j.jpsychores.2017.07.005.
87. Agnieszka A. Borowiec and Wojciech Drygas, "Work-Life Balance and Mental

and Physical Health Among Warsaw Specialists, Managers and Entrepreneurs," *International Journal of Environmental Research and Public Health* 20, no. 1 (2023): 492, https://doi.org/10.3390/ijerph20010492; Okely et al., "The Interaction Between Stress and Positive Affect in Predicting Mortality."

88. Clifton B. Parker, "Embracing Stress Is More Important Than Reducing Stress, Stanford Psychologist Says," Stanford Report, May 7, 2015, https://news.stanford.edu/stories/2015/05/embracing-stress-is-more-important-than-reducing-stress,-stanford-psychologist-says.
89. Merna Attia et al., "Cognitive, Emotional, Physical, and Behavioral Stress-Related Symptoms and Coping Strategies Among University Students During the Third Wave of COVID-19 Pandemic," *Frontiers in Psychiatry* 13 (2022): 933981, https://doi.org/10.3389/fpsyt.2022.933981.
90. Christina Maslach and Michael P. Leiter, *The Burnout Challenge: Managing People's Relationships with Their Jobs* (Harvard University Press, 2022).
91. Sabine Sonnentag and Charlotte Fritz, "Endocrinological Processes Associated with Job Stress: Catecholamine and Cortisol Responses to Acute and Chronic Stressors," in *Employee Health, Coping and Methodologies*, vol. 5 of *Research in Occupational Stress and Well Being*, eds. Pamela L. Perrewé and Daniel C. Ganster (Emerald Group Publishing Limited, 2006), https://doi.org/10.1016/S1479-3555(05)05001-8.
92. Michael T. Osborne et al., "Disentangling the Links Between Psychosocial Stress and Cardiovascular Disease," *Circulation: Cardiovascular Imaging* 13, no. 8 (2020): e010931, https://doi.org/10.1161/CIRCIMAGING.120.010931.
93. William Shaw et al., "Stress Effects on the Body," American Psychological Association, November 1, 2018, https://www.apa.org/topics/stress/body.
94. American Psychiatric Association, *Diagnostic and Statistical Manual of Mental Disorders: DSM-5-TR* (American Psychiatric Association, 2022), 313–19.
95. American Psychiatric Association, *Diagnostic and Statistical Manual of Mental Disorders.*
96. Evangelia Giourou et al., "Complex Posttraumatic Stress Disorder: The Need to Consolidate a Distinct Clinical Syndrome or to Reevaluate Features of Psychiatric Disorders Following Interpersonal Trauma?," *World Journal of Psyciatry* 8, no. 1 (2018): 12–19, https://doi.org/10.5498/wjp.v8.i1.12.
97. National Center for PTSD, "Trauma Reminders: Triggers," U.S. Department of Veterans Affairs, last updated March 26, 2025, https://www.ptsd.va.gov/understand/what/trauma_triggers.asp.
98. National Center for PTSD, "Trauma Reminders: Triggers."
99. Center for Substance Abuse Treatment (US), "Understanding the Impact of Trauma," chap. 3 in *Trauma-Informed Care in Behavioral Health Services*, in *Treatment Improvement Protocol (TIP) Series*, no. 57 (Substance Abuse and

Mental Health Services Administration (US), 2014), https://www.ncbi.nlm.nih.gov/books/NBK207191/.

100. Eve Riachi et al., "Psychotherapists' Views on Triggering Factors for Psychological Disorders,"*Discover Psychology* 2, no. 44 (2022): 44, https://doi.org/10.1007/s44202-022-00058-y.
101. Bessel van der Kolk, *The Body Keeps the Score: Brain, Mind, and Body in the Healing of Trauma* (Penguin Books, 2014), 67.
102. van der Kolk, *The Body Keeps the Score*, 68.
103. *Strong's Lexicon*, "5117. topos," Bible Hub, accessed August 3, 2025, https://biblehub.com/greek/5117.htm.
104. Prerna Sharma et al., "Childhood Trauma, Emotional Regulation, Alexithymia, and Psychological Symptoms Among Adolescents: A Mediational Analysis," *Indian Journal of Psychological Medicine* (2024), https://doi.org/10.1177/02537176241258251.
105. Sharma et al., "Childhood Trauma, Emotional Regulation, Alexithymia, and Psychological Symptoms Among Adolescents."
106. Reza Tadayonnejad, "Exploring the Connection Between Trauma and Personality Disorders," *Neuroscience and Psychiatry: Open Access* 7, no. 6 (2024): 281–83, https://www.openaccessjournals.com/articles/exploring-the-connection-between-trauma-and-personality-disorders-18230.html.
107. Sharma et al., "Childhood Trauma, Emotional Regulation, Alexithymia, and Psychological Symptoms Among Adolescents."
108. Sharma et al., "Childhood Trauma, Emotional Regulation, Alexithymia, and Psychological Symptoms Among Adolescents."
109. Jon Finch, "How Does Trauma Affect Decision Making?" Centre for Clinical Psychology, July 8, 2024, https://ccp.net.au/how-does-trauma-affect-decision-making/.
110. American Psychological Association, "Resilience," APA, accessed April 25, 2025, https://www.apa.org/topics/resilience.
111. *Leaders and Trauma Today.*
112. Richard A. Swenson, *Margin: Restoring Emotional, Physical, Financial, and Time Reserves to Overloaded Lives*, revised edition (NavPress, 2004).
113. E. E. Werner and Ruth S. Smith, *Vulnerable, but Invincible: A Longitudinal Study of Resilient Children and Youth* (McGraw-Hill, 1982). Werner defined resilience as, "The capacity [of individuals] to cope effectively with the internal stresses of their vulnerabilities (such as labile patterns of autonomic reactivity, developmental imbalances, unusual sensitivities) and external stresses (such as illness, major losses, and dissolution of the family)" (59).
114. Ben Stein, quoted in Tony Dungy, *The Mentor Leader: Secrets to Building People and Teams That Win Consistently* (Tyndale House Publishers, 2010), 86.

115. Jessica Martino et al., *The Connection Prescription: Using the Power of Social Interactions and the Deep Desire for Connectedness to Empower Health and Wellness. American Journal of Lifestyle Medicine* 11, no. 6 (2015): 466–75, https://doi.org/10.1177/1559827615608788.
116. American Psychological Association, "Resilience," APA, accessed May 11, 2025, https://www.apa.org/topics/resilience.
117. Lauren M. Sippel et al., "Sources of Social Support and Trauma Recovery: Evidence for Bidirectional Associations from a Recently Trauma-Exposed Community Sample," *Behavioral Sciences (Basel, Switzerland)* 14, no. 4 (2024): 284. https://doi.org/10.3390/bs14040284.
118. *Leaders and Trauma Today.*
119. Raheel Mashtaq, "Relationship Between Loneliness, Psychiatric Disorders and Physical Health?: A Review on the Psychological Aspects of Loneliness," *Journal of Clinical and Diagnostic Research* 8, no. 9 (2014): WE01–WE04, https://doi.org/10.7860/JCDR/2014/10077.4828.
120. Martino et al., *The Connection Prescription.*
121. Martino et al., *The Connection Prescription.*
122. Oxford Reference, "Mother Teresa," Oxford University Press, accessed July 15, 2025, https://www.oxfordreference.com/display/10.1093/acref/9780191843730.001.0001/q-oro-ed5-00010799.
123. *Leaders and Trauma Today.*
124. National Scientific Council on the Developing Child, "Young Children Develop in an Environment of Relationships: Working Paper No. 1," (Center on the Developing Child at Harvard University, 2004), https://developingchild.harvard.edu/resources/working-paper/wp1/.
125. *Leaders and Trauma Today.*
126. Nemanja Jovancic, "67 Zig Ziglar Quotes to Motivate Your Marketing and Sales Efforts," LeadQuizzes, December 24, 2018, https://www.leadquizzes.com/blog/zig-ziglar-quotes/.
127. T. Bryant-Davis and E. C. Wong, "Faith to Move Mountains: Religious Coping, Spirituality, and Interpersonal Trauma Recovery," *American Psychologist* 68, no. 8 (2013): 675–84, https://doi.org/10.1037/a0034380.
128. John C. Maxwell, *Winning with People: Discover the People Principles That Work for You Every Time* (Thomas Nelson, 2004), 47.
129. Jeffrey E. Auerbach, "The Rising Demand for Executive Coaches: The World's Most Famous CEOs Speak Out," College of Executive Coaching, August 12, 2024, https://www.executivecoachcollege.com/research-and-publications/rising-demand-for-executive-coaches.php.
130. Whitney Hopler, "Famous Quotes on Coaching for Leaders," Center for the Advancement of Well-Being, George Mason University, accessed May 7,

2025, https://wellbeing.gmu.edu/famous-quotes-on-coaching-for-leaders/.
131. *Leaders and Trauma Today.*
132. Kati Morton, *Traumatized: Identify, Understand, and Cope with PTSD and Emotional Stresses* (Hachette, 2021), 221.
133. Morton, *Traumatized*, 222–23.
134. Jim Collins, *Good to Great: Why Some Companies Make the Leap and Others Don't* (HarperCollins, 2001), 45.
135. John Baker, *Life's Healing Choices: Freedom from Your Hurts, Hang-ups, and Habits* (Howard, 2007), 111–12.
136. Jordan B. Peterson, *12 Rules for Life: An Antidote to Chaos* (Random House, 2018), 82–83.
137. Chris Hodges, *Out of The Cave: Stepping into the Light When Depression Darkens What You See* (Thomas Nelson, 2021), 204–5.
138. Seth Downland, "An Evangelistic Band of Brothers: Five Friends Who Helped Billy Graham Set—and Stay—His Course," *Christian History Magazine* 111 (2014), accessed July 2, 2025, https://christianhistoryinstitute.org/magazine/article/an-evangelistic-band-of-brothers.
139. Paul Dreschler, quoted in Aysha Frost, "The Ultimate List of Happiness and Wellbeing at Work Quotes," Haptivate, November 9, 2024, https://haptivate.co.uk/blog/the-ultimate-list-of-happiness-wellbeing-at-work-quotes/.
140. Tamara Bhandari, "Mind-Body Connection Is Built into Brain, Study Suggests," Washington University School of Medicine in St. Louis, April 19, 2023, https://medicine.wustl.edu/news/mind-body-connection-is-built-into-brain-study-suggests/.
141. Robert Sanders, "New Evidence That Chronic Stress Predisposes the Brain to Mental Illness," UC Berkeley Research News, February 11, 2014, https://vcresearch.berkeley.edu/news/new-evidence-chronic-stress-predisposes-brain-mental-illness.
142. Michael D. Nelson and Alecia M. Tumpap, "Posttraumatic Stress Disorder Symptom Severity Is Associated with Left Hippocampal Volume Reduction: A Meta-Analytic Study," *CNS Spectrums* 22, no. 4 (2017): 363–72, https://doi.org/10.1017/S1092852916000833.
143. Kelsey-Seybold Clinic, "Hormonal Imbalance: The Stress Effect," Kelsey-Seybold Clinic, May 21, 2022, accessed April 25, 2025, https://www.kelsey-seybold.com/your-health-resources/blog/hormonal-imbalance-the-stress-effect; S. B. Abraham et al., "Cortisol, Obesity, and the Metabolic Syndrome: A Cross-Sectional Study of Obese Subjects and Review of the Literature," *Obesity* 21, no. 1 (2013): E105–E117, https://doi.org/10.1002/oby.20083.
144. Hedy Marks and Lori M. King, "Stress Symptoms," WebMD, accessed April

25, 2025, https://www.webmd.com/balance/stress-management/stress-symptoms-effects_of-stress-on-the-body.

145. Lynette L. Craft and Frank M. Perna, "The Benefits of Exercise for the Clinically Depressed," *Primary Care Companion* to *Journal of Clinical Psychiatry* 6, no. 3 (2004): 104–11, https://doi.org/10.4088/pcc.v06n0301.
146. Kirk I. Erickson et al., "The Aging Hippocampus: Interactions Between Exercise, Depression, and BDNF," *The Neuroscientist* 18, no. 1 (2011): 82–97, https://doi.org/10.1177/1073858410397054.
147. Eva Selhub, "Nutritional Psychiatry: Your Brain on Food," Harvard Health Publishing, September 18, 2022, https://www.health.harvard.edu/blog/nutritional-psychiatry-your-brain-on-food-201511168626.
148. Luciana Besedovsky et al., "Sleep and Immune Function," *Pflugers Archive—European Journal of Physiology* 463 (2012): 121–37, https://doi.org/10.1007/s00424-011-1044-0.
149. PTSD UK, "Trauma: It's More Than Just 'Fight or Flight,'" PTSD UK (blog), accessed August 4, 2025, https://www.ptsduk.org/its-so-much-more-than-just-fight-or-flight/.
150. Habib Yaribeygi et al., "The Impact of Stress on Body Function: A Review," *EXCLI Journal* 16 (2017): 1057–72, https://doi.org/10.17179/excli2017-480.
151. Xiao Ma et al., "The Effect of Diaphragmatic Breathing on Attention, Negative Affect and Stress in Healthy Adults," *Frontiers in Psychology* 8, (2017): 874, https://doi.org/10.3389/fpsyg.2017.00874.
152. Yaribeygi et al., "The Impact of Stress on Body Function."
153. Rónán Doherty et al., "The Sleep and Recovery Practices of Athletes," *Nutrients* 13, no. 4 (2021): 1330, https://doi.org/10.3390/nu13041330.
154. Susan Cunningham, "Rest and Recovery Are Critical for Athletes of All Ages from Students to Pros to Older Adults," UC Health, March 31, 2025, accessed April 25, 2025, https://www.uchealth.org/today/rest-and-recovery-for-athletes-physiological-psychological-well-being/.
155. Erickson et al., "The Aging Hippocampus."
156. Craft and Perna, "The Benefits of Exercise for the Clinically Depressed."
157. Kirk I. Erickson et al., "Exercise Training Increases Size of Hippocampus and Improves Memory," *Proceedings of the National Academy of Sciences of the United States of America* 108, no. 7 (2011): 3017–22, https://doi.org/10.1073/pnas.1015950108.
158. Mami Sakurai et al., "Static Stretching Combined with Conscious Slower Breathing May Increase Parasympathetic Activity and Reduce Stress in Adult Women," *Health* 16, no. 3 (2024): 242–56, https://doi.org/10.4236/health.2024.163020.
159. Craft and Perna, "The Benefits of Exercise for the Clinically Depressed."

160. Catherine Woodyard, "Exploring the Therapeutic Effects of Yoga and Its Ability to Increase Quality of Life," *International Journal of Yoga* 4, no. 2 (2011): 49–54, https://doi.org/10.4103/0973-6131.85485.
161. Tamaki Amano and Motomi Toichi, "The Role of Alternating Bilateral Stimulation in Establishing Positive Cognition in EMDR Therapy: A Multi-Channel Near-Infrared Spectroscopy Study," *PLOS ONE* 11, no. 10 (2016): e0162735, https://doi.org/10.1371/journal.pone.0162735; Mathew G. Fetzner and Gordon J. G. Asmundson, "Aerobic Exercise Reduces Symptoms of Posttraumatic Stress Disorder: A Randomized Controlled Trial," *Cognitive Behavioral Therapy* 44, no. 4 (2015): 301–13, https://doi.org/10.1080/16506073.2014.916745; Aditya Mahindru et al., "Role of Physical Activity on Mental Health and Well-Being: A Review," *Cureus* 15, no. 1 (2023): e33475, https://doi.org/10.7759/cureus.33475; Simon Rosenbaum et al., "Physical Activity in the Treatment of Post-Traumatic Stress Disorder: A Systematic Review and Meta-Analysis," *Psychiatry Research* 230, no. 2 (2015): 130–36, https://doi.org/10.1016/j.psychres.2015.10.017.
162. Francine Shapiro, *Eye Movement Desensitization and Reprocessing (EMDR) Therapy: Basic Principles, Protocols, and Procedures*, 3rd ed. (Guilford Press, 2018).
163. Harvard T. H. Chan School of Public Health, "What Should I Eat?" The Nutrition Source, accessed April 25, 2025, https://nutritionsource.hsph.harvard.edu/what-should-you-eat/.
164. Hellas Cena and Philip C. Calder, "Defining a Healthy Diet: Evidence for The Role of Contemporary Dietary Patterns in Health and Disease," *Nutrients* 12, no. 2 (2020): 334, https://doi.org/10.3390/nu12020334.
165. James J. DiNicolantonio and James H. O'Keefe, "The Importance of Marine Omega-3s for Brain Development and the Prevention and Treatment of Behavior, Mood, and Other Brain Disorders," *Nutrients* 12, no. 8 (2020): 2333, https://doi.org/10.3390/nu12082333.
166. Helen Macpherson et al., "The Effects of Four-Week Multivitamin Supplementation on Mood in Healthy Older Women: A Randomized Controlled Trial," *Evidence-based Complementary and Alternative Medicine* (2016): 3092828, https://doi.org/10.1155/2016/3092828; Mary L. Fantacone et al., "The Effect of a Multivitamin and Mineral Supplement on Immune Function in Healthy Older Adults: A Double-Blind, Randomized, Controlled Trial," *Nutrients* 12, no. 8 (2020): 2447, https://doi.org/10.3390/nu12082447.
167. Habib Yaribeygi et al., "The Impact of Stress on Body Function: A Review," *EXCLI Journal* 16 (2017): 1057–72, https://doi.org/10.17179/excli2017-480.
168. Barry M. Popkin et al., "Water, Hydration, and Health," *Nutrition*

Reviews 68, no. 8 (2010): 439–58, https://doi.org/10.1111/j.1753-4887.2010.00304.x.

169. Cena and Calder, "Defining a Healthy Diet."
170. Jaime Uribarri et al., "Advanced Glycation End Products in Foods and a Practical Guide to Their Reduction in the Diet," *Journal of the American Dietetics Association* 110, no. 6 (2010): 911–16.e12, https://doi.org/10.1016/j.jada.2010.03.018.
171. Paula Alhola and Päivi Polo-Kantola, "Sleep Deprivation: Impact on Cognitive Performance," *Neuropsychiatric Disease and Treatment* 3, no. 5 (2007): 553–67, PMID: 19300585.
172. Harvard Medical School Division of Sleep Medicine, "Sleep and Health Education Program," accessed April 25, 2025, https://sleep.hms.harvard.edu/education-training/public-education/sleep-and-health-education-program/sleep-health-education-87.
173. Eric Suni, "How Much Sleep Do You Need?," updated July 11, 2025, accessed August 4, 2025, https://www.sleepfoundation.org/how-sleep-works/how-much-sleep-do-we-really-need.
174. Alhola and Polo-Kantola, "Sleep Deprivation."
175. Alhola and Polo-Kantola, "Sleep Deprivation."
176. Jake Newby, "The Benefits of Sleeping in a Dark Room," MI Blue Daily, April 5, 2025, accessed April 25, 2025, https://www.bcbsm.mibluedaily.com/stories/health-and-wellness/the-benefits-of-sleeping-in-a-dark-room.
177. Luciana Besedovsky et al., "Sleep and Immune Function," *Pflugers Archive—European Journal of Physiology* 463 (2012): 121–37, https://doi.org/10.1007/s00424-011-1044-0.
178. Washington State University, "Increasing Sleep Time After Trauma Could Ease Ill Effects," WSU Insider, October 22, 2020, https://news.wsu.edu/press-release/2020/10/22/increasing-sleep-time-trauma-ease-ill-effects/.
179. David S. Black and George M. Slavich, "Mindfulness Meditation and the Immune System: A Systematic Review of Randomized Controlled Trials," *Annals of the New York Academy of Sciences* 1373, no. 1 (2016): 13–24, https://doi.org/10.1111/nyas.12998.
180. Craft and Perna, "The Benefits of Exercise for the Clinically Depressed."
181. Richard J. Foster, *Celebration of Discipline, Special Anniversary Edition: The Path to Spiritual Growth* (HarperOne, 2018), 28.
182. Xiao Ma et al., "The Effect of Diaphragmatic Breathing on Attention, Negative Affect and Stress in Healthy Adults," *Frontiers in Psychology* 8 (2017): 874, https://doi.org/10.3389/fpsyg.2017.00874.
183. Balban, M. Y., Neri, E., Kogon, M. M., Weed, L., Nouriani, B., Jo, B., Holl, G., Zeitzer, J. M., Spiegel, D., & Huberman, A. D. (2023). Brief

structured respiration practices enhance mood and reduce physiological arousal. Cell reports. Medicine, 4(1), 100895. https://doi.org/10.1016/j.xcrm.2022.100895.

184. Catherine Woodyard, "Exploring the Therapeutic Effects of Yoga and Its Ability to Increase Quality of Life," *International Journal of Yoga* 4, no. 2 (2011): 49–54, https://doi.org/10.4103/0973-6131.85485.
185. Razia A. G. Khammissa et al., "Burnout Phenomenon: Neurophysiological Factors, Clinical Features, and Aspects of Management," *Journal of International Medical Research* 50, no. 9 (2022), https://doi.org/10.1177/03000605221106428.
186. Greg Salciccioli, *The Enemies of Excellence: 7 Reasons Why We Sabotage Success* (Crossroad Publishing Company, 2011), 37.
187. *Leaders and Trauma Today.*
188. Heryanto et al., "The Influence of Spiritual Leadership on Emotional Intelligence Moderated and Intervened by Self-Management," *Academic Journal of Interdisciplinary Studies* 12, no. 2 (2023): 123–34, https://doi.org/10.36941/ajis-2025-0013.
189. The Hebrew term translated as "excellent spirit" is *(rûach yattîrâh)* רוּחַ יַתִּיר.
190. David Green with Dean Merrill, *More Than a Hobby: How a $600 Startup Became America's Home and Craft Superstore* (Thomas Nelson, 2005), 46.
191. Noah Brooks, "Personal Recollections of Abraham Lincoln," *Harper's New Monthly Magazine*, July 1865, 230.
192. Emory University, "Psychologist Sees Benefits of Prayer, Meditation on Mental Health," Emory News Center, August 26, 2013, https://news.emory.edu/stories/2013/08/spirited_psychologist_sees_benefits_of_prayer/campus.html.
193. Amy B. Wachholtz and Kenneth I. Pargament, "Is Spirituality a Critical Ingredient of Meditation? Comparing the Effects of Spiritual Meditation, Secular Meditation, and Relaxation on Spiritual, Psychological, Cardiac, and Pain Outcomes," *Journal of Behavioral Medicine* 28, no. 4 (2005): 369–84, https://doi.org/10.1007/s10865-005-9008-5.
194. Andrew B. Newberg, "The Neurotheology Link: An Intersection Between Spirituality and Health," *Alternative and Complementary Therapies* 21, no. 1 (2015): 13–17, https://doi.org/10.1089/act.2015.21102.
195. Simranjeet Kaur et al., "From Struggle to Strength: The Therapeutic Potential of Gratitude Journaling for Student Mental Health," *Journal of Poetry Therapy* (2025): 1–16, https://doi.org/10.1080/08893675.2025.2457621; Joshua M. Smyth et al., "Online Positive Affect Journaling in the Improvement of Mental Distress and Well-Being in General Medical Patients with Elevated Anxiety Symptoms: A Preliminary Randomized Controlled Trial," *JMIR*

Mental Health 5, no. 4 (2018): e11290, https://doi.org/10.2196/11290.

196. Christopher N. Cascio et al., "Self-Affirmation Activates Brain Systems Associated with Self-Related Processing and Reward and Is Reinforced by Future Orientation," *Social Cognitive and Affective Neuroscience* 11, no. 4 (2016): 621–29, https://doi.org/10.1093/scan/nsv136.
197. Gang Wu et al., "Understanding Resilience," *Frontiers in Behavioral Neuroscience* 7 (2013): 10, https://doi.org/10.3389/fnbeh.2013.00010.
198. Norman Doidge, *The Brain That Changes Itself: Stories of Personal Triumph from the Frontiers of Brain Science* (Viking, 2007), 212.
199. Karina K. L. Mak et al., "Impostor Phenomenon Measurement Scales: A Systematic Review," *Frontiers in Psychology* 10 (2019): 671, https://doi.org/10.3389/fpsyg.2019.00671.
200. James Clear, "3-2-1: On Friendship, the Secret to Focus, and How to Cultivate a Good Life," *3-2-1 Newsletter*, December 21, 2023, https://jamesclear.com/3-2-1/december-21-2023.
201. Marcus Aurelius, *Meditations*, trans. George Long (Modern Library, 2002), 6.8.
202. Siri Kazilionis, "Trials to Triumphs: A Conceptual Integration of Resilience and Leadership" (2023). *CMC Senior Theses* (2023), 3526, https://scholarship.claremont.edu/cmc_theses/3526.
203. Kazilionis, "Trials to Triumphs."
204. Kazilionis, "Trials to Triumphs."
205. Katja M. Friederichs et al., "The Benefits of Prosocial Power Motivation in Leadership: Action Orientation Fosters a Win-Win," *PLOS ONE* 18, no. 7 (2023): e0287394, https://doi.org/10.1371/journal.pone.0287394.
206. Stephanie Watson, "Serotonin: The Natural Mood Booster," Harvard Health Publishing, November 20, 2023, https://www.health.harvard.edu/mind-and-mood/serotonin-the-natural-mood-booster.
207. Mental Health America, "What Are Endorphins?," Mental Health America, accessed May 8, 2025, https://mhanational.org/resources/what-are-endorphins/.
208. John P Grogan et al., "Dopamine Promotes Instrumental Motivation, but Reduces Reward-Related Vigour," *eLife* 9 (2020): e58321, https://doi.org/10.7554/eLife.58321.
209. Razia A. G. Khammissa et al., "Burnout Phenomenon: Neurophysiological Factors, Clinical Features, and Aspects of Management," *Journal of International Medical Research* 50, no. 9 (2022), https://doi.org/10.1177/03000605221106428.
210. Kristen L. Knutson et al., "The Metabolic Consequences of Sleep Deprivation," *Sleep Medicine Reviews* 11, no. 3 (2007): 163–78, https://doi.

org/10.1016/j.smrv.2007.01.002.

211. Christina Maslach and Michael P. Leiter, *The Truth About Burnout: How Organizations Cause Personal Stress and What to Do About It* (San Francisco: Jossey-Bass, 1997).
212. Alex M. Wood, John Maltby, Raphael Gillett, P. Alex Linley, and Stephen Joseph, "The Role of Gratitude in the Development of Social Support, Stress, and Depression: Two Longitudinal Studies," Journal of Research in Personality 42 (2008): 854–71.
213. Barbara L. Fredrickson, Michele M. Tugade, Christian E. Waugh, and Gregory R. Larkin, "What Good Are Positive Emotions in Crises? A Prospective Study of Resilience and Emotions Following the Terrorist Attacks on the United States on September 11th, 2001," *Journal of Personality and Social Psychology, 84, no. 2:* 365–76.
214. Wood et al., "The Role of Gratitude."
215. Jon Gordon, "The Power of Thank You," https://jongordon.com/positivetip/powerofthankyou.html.
216. Walter Brueggemann, *Sabbath as Resistance: Saying No to the Culture of Now* (John Knox Press, 2017), 29.
217. Peter Scazzero, *The Emotionally Healthy Leader: How Transforming Your Inner Life Will Deeply Transform Your Church, Team, and the World* (Zondervan, 2015), 144.
218. Scazzero, *The Emotionally Healthy Leader*, 145.
219. Shiv Shanker et al., "Chronic Restraint Stress Induces Serotonin Transporter Expression in the Rat Adrenal Glands," *Molecular and Cellular Endocrinology* 518 (2020): 110935, https://doi.org/10.1016/j.mce.2020.110935.
220. Søren Kierkegaard, *For Self-Examination*, trans. Howard V. Hong and Edna H. Hong (Princeton University Press, 1990), 47–48.
221. Mindsera, "Benefits of Journaling: The Science of Reflection," Mindsera, accessed May 30, 2025, https://www.mindsera.com/articles/benefits-of-journaling-the-science-of-reflection; James W. Pennebaker, "Expressive Writing in Psychological Science," *Perspectives on Psychological Science* 13, no. 2 (2017): 226–29, https://doi.org/10.1177/1745691617707315.
222. Wayne Cordeiro, *Leading on Empty: Refilling Your Tank and Renewing Your Passion* (Bethany House Publishers, 2010), 89.
223. Heanoy, E. Z., & Brown, N. R. (2024). Impact of Natural Disasters on Mental Health: Evidence and Implications. Healthcare (Basel, Switzerland), 12(18), 1812. https://doi.org/10.3390/healthcare1218181.2
224. *Leaders and Trauma Today.*
225. s.v. "מַכְאֹב (*makʾōb*)," in *A Concise Hebrew and Aramaic Lexicon of the Old Testament: Based on the First, Second, and Third Editions of Koehler-*

Baumgartner, ed. William L. Holladay (Grand Rapids, MI: Eerdmans, 1971).

226. Cleveland Clinic, "Limbic System," Cleveland Clinic, last reviewed April 6, 2024, accessed May 8, 2025, https://my.clevelandclinic.org/health/body/limbic-system.
227. Laurel Boyd, LMFT and LPC (Renewal Counseling), interview with the author, October 28, 2019.
228. Laurel Boyd, LMFT and LPC (Renewal Counseling), interview with the author, October 28, 2019.
229. Andrew B. Newberg, "The Neurotheology Link: An Intersection Between Spirituality and Health," *Alternative and Complementary Therapies* 21, no. 1 (2015): 13–17, https://doi.org/10.1089/act.2015.21102; René Muller, "Neurotheology: Are We Hardwired for God?," *Psychiatric Times* 25, no. 6 (2008), https://www.psychiatrictimes.com/view/neurotheology-are-we-hard-wired-god.
230. Michael Liedke, "Neurophysiological Benefits of Worship," *The Journal of Biblical Foundations of Faith and Learning* 3, no. 1 (2018): 22, https://knowledge.e.southern.edu/jbffl/vol3/iss1/22.
231. Liedke, "Neurophysiological Benefits of Worship."
232. s.v. "30.22 *σωφρονέω* (*sōphroneō*)," in *Greek-English Lexicon of the New Testament: Based on Semantic Domains,* ed. Johannes P. Louw and Eugene A. Nida, 2nd ed. (New York: United Bible Societies, 1989), 1:351–52.
233. Archibald Hart, *Adrenaline and Stress: The Exciting New Breakthrough That Helps You Overcome Stress Damage* (Thomas Nelson, 1995).
234. *Leaders and Trauma Today.*
235. s.v. "23.136 ἰάομαι (*iaomai*); ἴασις (*iasis*); σῴζω (*sōzō*); διασῴζω (*diasōzō*)," in *Greek-English Lexicon of the New Testament: Based on Semantic Domains,* ed. Johannes P. Louw and Eugene A. Nida, 2nd ed. (New York: United Bible Societies, 1989), 1:268.
236. Blair Paley and Nastassia J. Hajal, "Conceptualizing Emotion Regulation and Coregulation as Family-Level Phenomena," *Clinical Child and Family Psychology Review* 25, no. 1 (2022): 19–43, https://doi.org/10.1007/s10567-022-00378-4.
237. Brain and Behavior Research Foundation, "PTSD Trauma Memories Are Not Represented in the Brain Like Other Memories, Study Suggests," Brain and Behavior Research Foundation, February 29, 2024, accessed May 4, 2025, https://bbrfoundation.org/content/ptsd-trauma-memories-are-not-represented-brain-other-memories-study-suggests.
238. Simone Schnall et al., "Social Support and the Perception of Geographical Slant," *Journal of Experimental Social Psychology* 44, no. 5 (2008): 1246–55, https://doi.org/10.1016/j.jesp.2008.04.011.

239. Caroline Kettlewell, "Jack Needs Jill to Get Up the Hill," *Virginia Magazine*, 2022, accessed May 4, 2025, https://uvamagazine.org/articles/jack_needs_jill_to_get_up_the_hill.
240. Bessel van der Kolk, *The Body Keeps the Score: Brain, Mind, and Body in the Healing of Trauma* (Penguin Books, 2014), 212.
241. Angela Sweeney et al., "A Paradigm Shift: Relationships in Trauma-Informed Mental Health Services," *BJPsych Advances* 24, no. 5 (2018): 319–33, https://doi.org/10.1192/bja.2018.29.
242. Ryan J. Herringa, "Trauma, PTSD, and the Developing Brain," *Current Psychiatry Reports* 19, no. 10 (2017): 69, https://doi.org/10.1007/s11920-017-0825-3.
243. D. Cross et al., "Neurobiological Development in the Context of Childhood Trauma," *Clinical Psychology*: Science and Practice 24, no. 10 (2017): 111–24, https://doi.org/10.1111/cpsp.12198.
244. Van der Kolk, *The Body Keeps the Score*, 212.
245. *Leaders and Trauma Today.*
246. Kate Hudgins and Steven William Durost, *Experiential Therapy from Trauma to Post-Traumatic Growth: Therapeutic Spiral Model Psychodrama* (Spring Nature, 2022).
247. Tamaki Amano and Motomi Toichi, "The Role of Alternating Bilateral Stimulation in Establishing Positive Cognition in EMDR Therapy: A Multi-Channel Near-Infrared Spectroscopy Study," *PLOS ONE* 11, no. 10 (2016): e0162735, https://doi.org/10.1371/journal.pone.0162735.
248. Marie Kuhfuß et al., "Somatic Experiencing—Effectiveness and Key Factors of a Body-Oriented Trauma Therapy: A Scoping Literature Review," *European Journal of Psychotraumatology* 12, no. 1 (2021): 1929023, https://doi.org/10.1080/20008198.2021.1929023.
249. Ruud A. Jongedijk, "Narrative Exposure Therapy: An Evidence-Based Treatment for Multiple and Complex Trauma," *European Journal of Psychotraumatology* 5, no. 1 (2014): 26522, https://doi.org/10.3402/ejpt.v5.26522.
250. Fabio D'Antoni et al., "Psychotherapeutic Techniques for Distressing Memories: A Comparative Study between EMDR, Brainspotting, and Body Scan Meditation," *International Journal of Environmental Research and Public Health* 19, no. 3 (2022), https://doi.org/10.3390/ijerph19031142.
251. *Leaders and Trauma Today.*
252. Maren Westphal and George A. Bonanno, "Posttraumatic Growth and Resilience to Trauma: Different Sides of the Same Coin or Different Coins?," *Applied Psychology* 56, no. 3 (2007): 417–27, https://doi.org/10.1111/j.1464-0597.2007.00298.x.

253. Westphal and Bonanno, "Posttraumatic Growth and Resilience to Trauma."
254. Westphal and Bonanno, "Posttraumatic Growth and Resilience to Trauma."
255. *Britannica*, "Abraham Lincoln," last updated May 5, 2025, https://www.britannica.com/biography/Abraham-Lincoln.
256. Westphal and Bonanno, "Posttraumatic Growth and Resilience to Trauma."
257. Siang-Yang Tan, "Resilience and Posttraumatic Growth: Empirical Evidence and Clinical Applications from a Christian Perspective," *Journal of Psychology and Christianity* 32, no. 4 (2013): 358–64.
258. R Jetley , E Jallat and D Wallace "Post-Traumatic Stress Disorder or Post-Traumatic Stress Injury: What's in a name?" In History Issue Volume 28 No. 1 https://doi-ds.org/doilink/10.2022-79591933/JMVH Vol 28 No 1
259. Samantha Brooks et al., "Psychological Resilience and Post-Traumatic Growth in Disaster-Exposed Organisations: Overview of the Literature," *BMJ Military Health* 166, no. 1 (2020): 52–56, https://doi.org/10.1136/jramc-2017-000876.
260. Frank J. Infurna and Eranda Jayawickreme, "Fixing the Growth Illusion: New Directions for Research in Resilience and Posttraumatic Growth," *Current Directions in Psychological Science* 28, no. 2 (2019): 152–58, https://doi.org/10.1177/0963721419827017.
261. Stephen Z. Levine et al., "Examining the Relationship Between Resilience and Posttraumatic Growth," *Journal of Traumatic Stress* 22, no. 4 (2009): 282–86, https://doi.org/10.1002/jts.20409.
262. Wenjie Duan et al., "Relationships Among Trait Resilience, Virtues, Post-Traumatic Stress Disorder, and Post-Traumatic Growth," *PLOS ONE* 10, no. 5 (2015): e0125707, https://doi.org/10.1371/journal.pone.0125707.
263. *Leaders and Trauma Today.*
264. Alan Ewert and Sharon Tessneer, "Psychological Resilience and Posttraumatic Growth: An Exploratory Analysis," *Journal of Experiential Education* 42, no. 3 (2019): 280–96, https://doi.org/10.1177/1053825919859027.
265. Taylor Elam and Kanako Taku, "Differences Between Posttraumatic Growth and Resiliency: Their Distinctive Relationships with Empathy and Emotion Recognition Ability," *Frontiers in Psychology* 13 (2022): 825161, https://doi.org/10.3389/fpsyg.2022.825161.
266. William Steele and Caelan Kuban, "Trauma-Informed Resilience and Posttraumatic Growth (PTG)," *Reclaiming Children and Youth* 20, no. 3 (2011): 44–46.
267. Michael S. Leeman et al., "Lifestyle, Coping Resources, and Trauma Symptoms: Predicting Post-Traumatic Growth," *The Journal of Individual Psychology* 79, no. 3 (2023): 218–39, https://dx.doi.org/10.1353/jip.2023.a909957.

268. Stephen Joseph, *What Doesn't Kill Us: The New Psychology of Posttraumatic Growth* (Basic Books, 2013).

269. Duan et al., "Relationships Among Trait Resilience, Virtues, Post-Traumatic Stress Disorder, and Post-Traumatic Growth."
270. Duan et al., "Relationships Among Trait Resilience, Virtues, Post-Traumatic Stress Disorder, and Post-Traumatic Growth."
271. Geyze Diniz et al., "The Effects of Gratitude Interventions: A Systematic Review and Meta-Analysis," *Einstein (Sao Paulo, Brazil)* 21 (2023): eRW0371, https://doi.org/10.31744/einstein_journal/2023RW0371.
272. Stephanie Nolasco, "Kidnapping Survivor Elizabeth Smart on Empowering Kids from Predators: 'Don't Be Afraid to Practice Screaming,'" Fox News, January 28, 2024, https://www.foxnews.com/us/kidnapping-survivor-elizabeth-smart-empowering-kids-predators-dont-be-afraid.
273. Jordan G., "Drew Brees to Deliver NATA 2018 Keynote," National Athletic Trainers' Association, April 19, 2018, https://www.nata.org/nata-now/articles/2018/04/drew-brees-deliver-nata-2018-keynote.
274. Drew Brees, *Coming Back Stronger: Unleashing the Hidden Power of Adversity* (Tyndale House Publishers, 2010), xxi.
275. Brees, *Coming Back Stronger*, 23.
276. Brees, *Coming Back Stronger*, 103.
277. Viktor E. Frankl, *Man's Search for Meaning*, trans. Ilse Lasch (Beacon Press, 2006), 113.
278. Samuel R. Chand, *Leadership Pain: The Classroom for Growth* (Thomas Nelson, 2015).